A Friend's and Relative's Guide to Supporting the Family with Autism

Ann Palmer

A Friend's and Relative's Guide to Supporting the Family with Autism

How Can I Help?

Foreword by Stephen M. Shore

Jessica Kingsley *Publishers*
London and Philadelphia

616.85882
PAL

First published in 2012
by Jessica Kingsley Publishers
116 Pentonville Road
London N1 9JB, UK
and
400 Market Street, Suite 400
Philadelphia, PA 19106, USA

www.jkp.com

Library of Congress Cataloging in Publication Data
A CIP catalog record for this book is available from the Library of Congress

British Library Cataloguing in Publication Data
A CIP catalogue record for this book is available from the British Library

ISBN 978 1 84905 877 3
eISBN 978 0 85700 567 0

Printed and bound in the United States

I dedicate this book to all my family members and friends who "got it." Thanks to all of you who understood what I was going through during the difficult times and were there to celebrate with me when things got better. Your support means the world to me.

CONTENTS

FOREWORD

The tag line of the title says it all: "How can I help?" The urge to support another person having a child with autism is strong; however, what can you do? In addition to processing their own emotions and expectations for their child, the family itself may be confused in what to do and conflicted in telling their friends and family about their child with autism. Written by a parent of a child with autism, this book will be a great support and comfort for families as well.

You've taken the first step by picking up this book by Ann Palmer—something my relatives and family friends would have found very useful when I was diagnosed on the autism spectrum, given a life sentence of institutionalization at a time when the label carried great shame. We have come far from a point of barely any resources for autism to easily accessing a torrent of information from millions of hits on an internet search engine.

"Autism" is familiar to many or even most people, but individuals remain at a loss for how they can help. A common saying in the autism community, "When a child has autism, the whole family has autism," may initially sound silly. However, it's important to realize that the entire family, including immediate and extended, is very much like a mobile that may be hanging above a baby's crib, in the lobby of a building, or in a museum. When one part of the mobile moves, all the other parts of the structure shift. The same happens to the family. Often mirroring the challenges in communication and social interaction of the child with autism, soon the family may find it more difficult to visit friends and family, and to engage in the community. More than ever at this time, they need the communication, support, and humanity that comes from interacting with others.

Being able to help starts with knowing what autism is—and what it isn't, as so skillfully portrayed in this book. Expertly combining scientific research with what the families themselves have experienced, Ann provides an efficient, complete pathway to understanding mealtimes, sleep schedules, going out in public, finances, and intra- and inter-family relationships, to name just a few of the facets of life that can be affected when a family has a child with autism.

With the artistry of a master chef, Ann Palmer creates a thick stew, chockfull of helpful suggestions for friends and relatives of families with autism, ranging from helping with laundry and running errands to bringing over a meal. For those who are geographically far away, support is as close as an email or phone to check in and to see where you might help. Another wise suggestion is that just being there to nonjudgmentally listen without saying a word can be very helpful. And to keep the stew from spoiling, Ann gently provides guidance and explanation as to what is not helpful—even if what you are doing seems supportive at the time. Finally, the "Top Ten Tips for Family Members and Friends" is a must read for those not having sufficient time to read the entire book and for those who wish to buttress the contents inside.

In this book you will find all the information you need to begin the first step in walking hand in hand alongside your friends and family as you join their journey in living with, providing meaningful support for, and making the world a better place for the autism community.

Here's where you can help.

Stephen M. Shore, Ed.D.
Assistant Professor of Special Education at Adelphi University
Internationally renowned author, consultant and presenter
on issues related to the autism spectrum

ACKNOWLEDGMENTS

I want to thank all of my fellow "autism parents," and their friends and family members, for contributing to this book. Thank you for sharing your personal experiences concerning your loved one with ASD. My autism friends have become a second family to me, and for that I will always be grateful.

Thank you to my husband Bobby for your excellent editing skills and for allowing me the freedom to quit my job and focus on doing what I love to do.

And thank you to Jessica Kingsley and her wonderful staff for their continuing support over the years.

INTRODUCTION

This is a book for anyone who cares about someone with an autism spectrum disorder or ASD. The incidence of ASD has increased dramatically since the 1980s, therefore the number of those who care about individuals with ASD has increased as well. We hear the words "autism" or "autism spectrum disorder" in the news frequently. If you do an online search for autism spectrum disorder, you may get over 3.5 million hits. Extensive research is being done all over the world as we try to learn more about ASD and its causes. An increasing number of movies and television programs include characters with an autism spectrum disorder. With all this publicity it is difficult to find anyone who has not heard about autism or who does not know someone personally who is affected.

Despite the overwhelming amount of information available, there is still a great deal of confusion and misunderstanding about ASD. It is a complicated disorder and often difficult to diagnose. No two individuals with ASD are the same; every person who has ASD is unique, with their own strengths and challenges. Every family's experience of living with ASD is different. Professionals working in the field of autism often disagree about the causes and what interventions are best. It is no surprise that people not working in the field and not living with ASD may have trouble fully understanding the disorder.

You may be reading this book because you are a grandparent, cousin, aunt or uncle of someone with ASD and want to do something to help. Maybe you are a longtime friend of the family, a neighbor, or a co-worker who just wants to understand. You may be reading this book because you are the parent of a newly diagnosed child with an autism spectrum disorder and want to know more about what other families are experiencing and how your family and friends can help you. This book is an effort to connect those of you living with autism with those of you who care about them. Sounds easy? It can be, but often is not.

FAMILY AND FRIENDS

In a perfect world our family and our friends provide us with the help we need when we go through difficult times in our lives. They are the "safe place" we can go to when there is nowhere else to go and no one else to talk to. Our family and our friends accept us no matter what, forgive our mistakes, and love us unconditionally. In a perfect world we can open up to our family and friends about our fears and our joys and know they will understand.

Over the many years that I've been working with families of children with autism, I've learned that family relationships are often not perfect and can be extremely complicated. Most of us are not fortunate enough to have the Waltons' kind of family relationships where everything is discussed out in the open and every conflict ends up with loving "good nights" at the end of the day. Our history with our families can be long and painful. We may have certain family members that we don't get along with or relationships that were damaged a long time ago. Improving those relationships may seem impossible. Physical distance, the passing of time, and misunderstandings may have gotten in the way of developing close relationships with our family members. Even if you have had a very rewarding, wonderful relationship with your family, the introduction of autism into the family can change things, sometimes for the better and sometimes for the worse.

The introduction of autism can also impact our relationships with friends. In our transient society today it is typical to be living far away from family and friendships may become our primary support system. Friendships give us a place to complain, to laugh, to rejoice, and to just be ourselves. And when something difficult, maybe devastating, changes our lives, our friends may be the first people we turn to for support. However, the complicated nature of living with ASD can also complicate our relationships with friends.

Research shows us that support from family and friends can be crucial for those living with someone with ASD. As I will discuss in Chapter 2, raising a child with ASD impacts every aspect of life and can cause an incredible amount of stress on the parents—emotional, physical, and financial. It can test the marriage and impact the lives of the siblings of the child with ASD. Having a support system that includes extended family members and friends can make a difference in how successful families are in coping with this experience.

> One of the most important things about a strong family network is that it gives us a safe haven—a place where we can allow ourselves to be vulnerable, to express our own pain, our dashed hopes and our fears. In turn, we are opening ourselves up and readying ourselves to receive assistance, feedback, encouragement and support—knowing that it comes from a caring place, from the family we know and trust. (Martin 2010, p.99)

As mentioned earlier, it may not be easy to develop these supportive relationships. There are many factors that can influence a parent's ability to reach out for support or to accept support when it is offered. It can also be very difficult for family members and friends to know what to say or how to help. Maintaining friendships can be difficult under the best of circumstances, and may be next to impossible for parents overwhelmed by the day-to-day struggles of living with autism.

Understanding seems to be the key. "Autism itself is not awful. Not understanding it, not having people around you who understand it, not getting the help that is surely out there for your child—that can be very awful" (Notbohm 2005, p.xvi). Many of the roadblocks to building supportive relationships come from a lack of understanding. People may not understand the diagnosis and how it affects the individual child. Or they may not understand what the parents are feeling when their child is diagnosed, and what kinds of reactions don't help. People may not understand the day-to-day difficulties of living with someone with autism, and the kinds of support that could help. And parents may not understand the pain, confusion, and frustration that extended family members and friends also may be feeling. One of the goals of this book is to help people understand so they can be there for each other.

MY PERSONAL EXPERIENCE

I care very much about someone with autism—my son, Eric. Our journey with autism began in 1985 when Eric was two years old. I don't remember a lot from that day I sat across the table from the speech clinician, awaiting the results from her speech and hearing assessment. I don't remember her name. I don't remember any of the official testing results. I don't remember anything she said after these six words, "Have you ever heard of autism?" I do remember that I cried quietly while she talked. I remember that I took Eric to the car, put him in his car seat, and sat and cried in the car. I know I somehow drove home and my Mom was there babysitting my daughter. I remember she said something like "Oh no, you've been crying! What happened?" I couldn't answer her. The walls had already gone up. Talking about it would allow the floodgates to open and I couldn't let that happen. I think I told her I'd tell her later and she left, confused and worried.

The next couple of weeks were a blur. I did all the things I needed to, like take care of the kids, my husband, the house; but I was in a fog. I felt a pain, deep inside of me. I would be doing something mundane like preparing dinner, and I would suddenly not be able to stand and would slide to the floor and cry. I couldn't control my emotions and felt like I had no control over my life.

I was eventually able to tell my mother and my sisters about what the speech clinician had said. There were some tears and lots of words of encouragement that it probably wasn't autism, everything will be fine, etc. I latched onto those statements, desperately trying to cling to any possibility that this couldn't be true. Even my son's pediatrician agreed that it wasn't autism (because Eric was talking) and quickly dismissed my concerns. As much as we wanted to believe what everyone was saying, my husband and I knew that autism was more than a possibility. We took Eric to a developmental pediatrician who was very knowledgeable about autism spectrum disorders. After a long and very thorough evaluation she confirmed that Eric did indeed have autism.

Soon after the diagnosis I started attending a local support group for mothers of children with autism and continued to find support there for many years. I met wonderful moms who were going through many of the same things I was experiencing. There were also moms there whose children were quite different from mine. But I learned from those mothers too and began to recognize that despite the differences in our children, we all had a very powerful connection and a shared understanding that I had not found anywhere else.

We would have a topic of discussion at each support group meeting and one of the recurring topics over the years was "the extended family." I remember sitting at the table and listening to one after another of the moms talk about family members who were making their lives miserable. One mom talked about her parent who didn't agree with the diagnosis and thought they should just spank their child more. One talked about the family members who stopped inviting them to family gatherings because of their child with autism. One shared the story of her sister who sent her every article from the newspaper about autism and asked why she wasn't doing that therapy with her child. I heard one mom talk about her in-laws who actually blamed her for their grandchild's autism. I was shocked at the stories I was hearing and the pain these mothers expressed. There were a few positive, inspiring stories of support from family members (including my own stories) but most were stories of difficult experiences. I was very surprised and confused about why this seemed to happen so often.

I know how much I needed my family's support, especially during the time immediately following the diagnosis when our life was such chaos and I had no idea what I was doing. I can't imagine how much harder my life would have been if my family had been adding stress to my life instead of helping me cope. I appreciate now how lucky I was. Eric's grandparents lived close by and tried their best to understand what we were going through and they did what they could to support us.

Despite the many difficulties that families experience that I will describe in this book, many of the stories of raising children with ASD are success stories. Our definition of success may have changed somewhat from the definition we had before our children were diagnosed, but they are still success stories. Most of those mothers attending the support group meetings with me many years ago would tell you now that their lives are much easier. They would tell you that their children are incredible adults with meaningful and productive lives. That future we were afraid of so many years ago at that mothers' support group, is now, and we find it very different from what we imagined.

My son Eric is a success story and I am incredibly proud of him and all he has accomplished. I attribute his success to many things, including the support we received from our family members and friends. Eric went from being an out-of-control, routine-obsessed three-year-old, to being a calm, flexible college graduate who lives in his own apartment and works a full-time job he enjoys. He still has autism, and always will. The autism still challenges him at times and makes his life different from the lives of most 29-year-olds. But that's okay because he is happy and I am content with who he is and the wonderful addition he has been to my life.

Eric has taught me that we can't predict the future for our children with ASD and we mustn't close doors to opportunities that are possible, but feel impossible (Palmer 2006). Your loved one on the autism spectrum may not accomplish the same things Eric has, but he or she will accomplish more than you can possibly imagine. With all the supports and strategies that are available, anything is possible.

SIMILARITIES AND DIFFERENCES IN EXPERIENCES

As you will read in Chapter 1, our children on the autism spectrum are similar in certain ways but different as well. The severity of the symptoms varies from person to person and within each individual child. They may have challenges in certain areas, but have great strengths in other areas. Because of this variety of symptoms, every experience of raising a child with ASD is going to be unique.

I may not be able to provide within this book that perfect match to your own personal experience with ASD. I have included a variety of personal stories and comments within this book; some won't apply at all to your situation with your loved one and some will hit very close to home. However, even if what you read doesn't describe your particular experience, it will help you understand the wide range of possibilities and challenges that families may face.

Individuals with ASD are often described in evaluations and reports as being mild, moderate or severe. Professionals may also use the phrase "high or low functioning" to describe the child's abilities or level of needs. Personally, I'm not crazy about any of these descriptors but I understand why they are used by professionals; and parents often encourage the use of these terms by their desire to know where their child falls on the autism spectrum. But these words often only confuse us more as we try to understand our loved one with ASD. These terms are not always accurate predictors of the future. For example, a child at three years old may be considered "moderately affected" by their autism and with therapies and treatment may end up making excellent progress and later be considered "mildly affected."

The term "high or low functioning" is also deceiving. There are individuals who are considered mildly affected or "high functioning" and are fairly independent in many ways but may at the same time be quite challenged. Some individuals with high functioning autism may have behaviors or anxieties that can seriously limit their ability to function in their daily lives. In other words, high functioning does not always mean easier. There are individuals with ASD who may be considered low functioning or intellectually impaired who live productive and happy lives. Parents, family members and friends should not be too focused on the terminology and should instead focus on the individual strengths and challenges of their loved one with ASD.

Along with the different levels of need that we see in our children with ASD, we also see different coping abilities for the parents and family. Every family's experience will be different and everyone's reaction to the diagnosis and to living with autism will vary. There is no right way to react, to grieve, or to reach acceptance. Some families live with extremely difficult situations and intense behaviors that disrupt their daily lives, while others find that living with autism makes less of an impact on their day-to-day lives. Some families have lots of support and resources available to them, while some are limited in their supports because of their geographical location and financial situation. Many parents are able to recognize their family's needs easily and will reach out for help and welcome that help when it is given. Other parents may not feel as comfortable accepting support. Whatever the situation you are in, I hope that you will find some information within this book that will help you understand and cope with the experience you are living.

PERSONAL PERSPECTIVES

Throughout this book I have included personal comments from parents of children with ASD, extended family members, and friends. They are the color commentary, so to speak, for this book. Some quotes were taken directly from the surveys I sent out and interviews I did and some were quoted from books and articles found during my research on this topic. My intention in including them was to provide the reader with many different perspectives in addition to my own. Hearing from others has opened my eyes to the wide range of emotions and experiences and will, I hope, provide the reader with a better understanding of life on this spectrum.

The personal accounts from people I contacted in the process of writing this book are just that, personal. For that reason I have not included identifying names in order to protect their anonymity. Where you may see names included, however, are in direct quotes taken from previously published articles and books.

DIAGNOSTIC CATEGORIES

There are multiple diagnostic categories used to diagnose individuals on the autism spectrum. I will be going into more detail about them in Chapter 1. Your loved one may be diagnosed with autism, Asperger syndrome, or pervasive developmental disorder—not otherwise specified (PDD-NOS). I have used the term autism spectrum disorder (ASD) throughout this book to include these diagnoses. I may also use the word "autism" at times as meaning autism spectrum disorders.

In Chapter 1 I have tried to give a general description of what ASD might look like, how it is diagnosed, and the current information available at the time of the publication of this book. This is a very general summary meant to be helpful to the lay person just learning about ASD. There are countless books and websites available with more detailed information. I have also included a section about different interventions that may be helpful to your loved one with ASD. I realize that not all of these interventions may be readily available where you live and not all treatments are beneficial to all children with ASD. Again, this is a general description of options to consider, knowing that you will need to do more research before choosing what is best for your loved one.

ABOUT THIS BOOK

This book is primarily for families and friends in the beginning stage of learning about this disorder and most newly diagnosed individuals on the autism spectrum will be children. I am aware that adolescents and adults are also being diagnosed with ASD and your connection with autism may be with this population. Many of the descriptions and examples included in this book will refer to coping with the diagnosis and the needs of a child with ASD, but this information should also be helpful to those connected to older individuals. The challenges that come from receiving a diagnosis and the experience of coping with this new information is universal in all families, no matter the age of the individual with ASD.

This is my third book and in many ways was the most difficult to write. Every aspect of this topic is complicated and packed with emotion. I realized during my writing that I can never describe all the possible scenarios that can complicate a relationship between parents of a child with ASD and their family members and friends. And I'm sure there are relationships that will never be repaired even with all the advice and strategies I may suggest. But I'm hopeful that, by reading this book, people will understand the importance of having support in this experience and appreciate those who are reaching out to help.

If you are a family member or friend of someone living with ASD, you may not realize how important your words and actions can be to a family struggling to understand what has happened to their life. A phone call, a note, a word of encouragement, or a simple act of listening can have a powerful impact on the person you care about who is living with autism. Thank you for caring enough to pick up this book and wanting to be important in the life of someone with autism spectrum disorder.

Chapter 1

UNDERSTANDING AUTISM SPECTRUM DISORDERS

Understanding autism spectrum disorders is not easy for anyone, so if you are struggling to understand it, you are definitely not alone. Despite more than 60 years of research, we still do not know all the causes of autism and there is currently no cure. There are many forms of treatment and therapies that we know can benefit individuals with autism but there is no consensus on the best treatment. What works for one child may not for another. Every individual with ASD is affected in different ways and to varying degrees. As we say in the autism world, "When you've met one child with autism, you've met *one* child with autism." Some individuals will have only a few autistic characteristics and some will display many. It often seems to parents that everything about ASD is confusing and that it's difficult to know what to believe.

The more things change, the more they stay the same. The four core realities that confronted us as new mothers in 1980 still confront new mothers today. There is no consensus on what causes autism. There is no universal agreement on what might cure autism. There is no widely-shared opinion on which education and treatment approach is most effective. And the decision on what course of action to take still rests with overwhelmed parents. (Morrell and Palmer 2006, p.13)

Despite all that we don't know, there are things we do know. We know that ASDs occur in all racial, ethnic, and socioeconomic groups. It is four times more likely to occur in boys than girls. In 2010 the Centers for Disease Control and Prevention (CDC) estimated that 1 in 80 boys and 1 in every 240 girls, or an average of 1 in 110 children in the United States, have an ASD (CDC 2010b). In 2009 the American Academy of Pediatrics found that the rate of parent-reported autism was 1 in every 91 children, and 1 in every 58 boys. It is the fastest growing developmental disability in the United States and is diagnosed more than diabetes, AIDS, and cancer combined. More than 1.5 million people in the United States have autism (Martin 2010).

HISTORY

When my son was first diagnosed in 1985, the incidence of autism was estimated at four or five out of every ten thousand births. Obviously there has been a sharp increase in the incidence but it is not clear why. Autism was probably misdiagnosed in the past, at least until the 1970s and 1980s when our understanding about the spectrum improved. Previously, more able people with ASD were often not diagnosed at all, while those more challenged were diagnosed as having mental retardation, not autism. Our greater awareness of the signs and symptoms of ASD have led to more individuals being diagnosed. This greater awareness has also facilitated diagnosis at a younger age, another factor possibly influencing the increase in reported incidence. Another contributing factor to the increase is that the definition of ASD has been broadened to include those with milder impairments and with Asperger syndrome.

The study of autism spectrum disorders is relatively new. Our understanding began in the 1940s. Leo Kanner, an Austrian psychiatrist at Johns Hopkins University, first described some peculiarities he had seen in 11 children in his practice. He used the term "early infantile autism" (Kanner 1943). Around the same time in 1944, Hans Asperger, a German pediatrician practicing at the university pediatric clinic in Vienna, noticed similar symptoms, though in a milder form, and called it "autistic psychopathy." Both Kanner and Asperger studied at the same university in Austria. Asperger died in 1980 and never knew that the condition Asperger syndrome would be named for him a few years later. His writings were in German and were pretty much ignored in English-speaking countries until Lorna Wing, a psychiatrist and physician in England, published an article describing it in 1981 (Frith 1991).

Kanner and Asperger helped open the door to our understanding of this complicated disorder. Unfortunately, there were also those that did not help and actually had a very negative impact on the history of autism. When I first learned about my son's autism, I went to my neighborhood library to find books related to autism. This was before the internet and the library was one of the few resources parents had. One book I found was *The Empty Fortress* (1967) by Bruno Bettelheim, an Austrian psychologist. He believed that autism in children was caused by "refrigerator mothers"—cold and unfeeling parents who made their children feel isolated and unloved. He had spent two years in concentration camps and compared the mental isolation of children with autism to prisoners of war.

Bettelheim's theories were accepted for 20 years and led to autism being considered a mental illness. Because his theories were so widely accepted, for years professionals when diagnosing autism would suggest that the child be institutionalized and that the parents receive psychotherapy. It was later discovered that Bettelheim worked in his family's lumber business and had a degree in art history. He had no qualifications to theorize about the causes of autism (Sicile-Kira 2004). However, his book was still on library shelves in 1985 and his inaccurate and prejudiced theories caused serious emotional distress to many families for many years.

CAUSES

Unfortunately, we still do not know all the causes of autism. We haven't discovered one exact cause of autism that operates for all children and in fact some experts believe there will eventually be multiple causes linked to autism (Shore and Rastelli 2006).

> Since genetic, infectious, neurological, immunological, and possible environmental influences have been implicated in autism, no one is naïve enough to suggest that any one cause will account for all cases of autism, nor that any one treatment or "cure" will be sufficient to deal with all of its manifestations. Autism and the enormous variability among individuals with autism might be better understood as a class of disorders. Solving the puzzle of autism will be like peeling an onion, one layer at a time. (Bristol-Power 2000, p.16)

One thing we do know is that genetic factors can increase a child's risk for having an autism spectrum disorder and it does run in some families (Stone and DiGeronimo 2006). There are many families with more than one child with autism. The Centers for Disease Control and Prevention estimated that parents who have a child with an ASD have a 2–8 percent chance of having a second child who is also affected (CDC 2010a). However, a more recent study by Sally Ozonoff and others showed that the sibling recurrence of autism spectrum disorder is substantially higher than previous estimates. They found that 18.7 percent of infants with at least one older sibling with ASD developed the disorder (Ozonoff *et al.* 2011). Sometimes a parent may discover that they themselves were misdiagnosed or not diagnosed with ASD but believe they have the condition. Also:

> ASDs tend to occur more often in people who have certain other medical conditions. About 10% of children with an ASD have an identifiable genetic disorder, such as Fragile X syndrome, tuberous sclerosis, Down syndrome and other chromosomal disorders. (CDC 2010b)

Some experts believe that anything that makes the central nervous system develop abnormally can cause autism. This would mean that autism can occur during fetal development, during birth, or after birth (Janzen 2003). The Centers for Disease Control and Prevention is looking at all possible risk factors before and after birth including genetic, environmental, pregnancy, and behavioral factors. For more information about the current research being done by the CDC on possible causes and risk factors, you can go to www.cdc.gov/ncbddd/autism/research.html.

If you have done any reading at all about autism, you have probably read about the controversy concerning immunizations and autism. There have been many studies looking at the relationship between vaccines and autism spectrum disorders. So far, the studies are showing that vaccines are *not* associated with autism. The article originally published in the British medical journal, *The Lancet,* stating there was a connection between autism and the vaccine for measles, mumps, and rubella was later withdrawn and the data declared false. The author has since lost his license to practice medicine. However, many parents continue to believe that their children developed autism symptoms as a result of immunizations and some families are choosing not to get their children vaccinated. The Inter-Agency Autism Coordinating Committee (IACC), a federal advisory committee consisting of both federal and public members, is working with the National Vaccine Advisory Committee on this important topic. For more information about vaccines and autism spectrum disorder, you can find multiple links listed on the CDC website.

Fortunately, our understanding about autism spectrum disorders has improved and we now know that it is a neurobiological, developmental disorder, not a mental or emotional disorder, and it is not caused by bad parenting. Autism affects the way the brain develops and causes differences in the way information is processed. It affects the ability to understand and use language to interact and relate to others. It affects the ability to respond to sensory stimuli such as pain, hearing, touch and taste. Children with ASD learn and think differently than neurotypically developing children (Janzen 2003).

As researchers continue to study autism and search for a cause or causes, we also have to wonder whether finding a cause may someday lead to a cure. There is an ongoing debate about curing autism. Those parents who struggle with raising a child with severe challenges or extremely taxing behaviors are understandably going to wish for a cure for this disorder. Our nature as parents directs us to do everything we can to rid our children of this condition that makes their lives so difficult. For our children who cannot communicate their views about this issue, we can't know how they feel about having ASD or if they support our efforts to diminish the autistic behaviors that affect their lives. We can only try to respect the right of individuals with ASD to be who they are (Morrell and Palmer 2006).

An increasing number of individuals on the autism spectrum are advocating for their rights to be who they are, and not who others expect them to be. Many feel there are benefits to being on the autism spectrum and they should be welcomed into the neurotypical world for the unique and creative views they can contribute. They eloquently make the point that they do not think of ASD as a disease, therefore they don't need a cure. Rather than trying to suppress certain autistic traits, they feel people in the neurotypical world should simply be more tolerant.

Jim Sinclair, a man with ASD speaking at the 1993 International Conference on Autism in Toronto, explains his perspective well:

> Look at your grief from our perspective... Autism isn't something a person has, or a "shell" that a person is trapped inside. There's no normal child hidden behind the autism. Autism is a way of being. It is *pervasive*; it colors every experience, every sensation, perception, thought, emotion, and encounter, every aspect of existence... It is not possible to separate the person from the autism. Therefore, when parents say, "I wish my child did not have autism," what they're really saying is "I wish the autistic child I have did not exist, and I had a different (non-autistic) child instead"... This is what we hear when you mourn over our existence. This is what we hear when you pray for a cure. (Sinclair 1993, p.1)

DIAGNOSIS AND SYMPTOMS

This leads us to a discussion of how ASD is diagnosed and what symptoms a child may have. First of all, there is no medical test like a blood test to diagnose autism spectrum disorders. Doctors must look at the child's developmental history and their behaviors in order to diagnose them. Parents are typically the first ones to have concerns or notice that something is different. They may see some unusual behaviors or see a delay in language or a delay in reaching developmental milestones. Studies have shown that about one-third of parents of children with ASD noticed a problem before the child turned the age of one and 80 percent of parents saw problems by age two (CDC 2010a).

However, first time parents may not pick up on the differences, especially if the differences are subtle. In those cases, it may be a screening done during a regular checkup with the pediatrician that brings up the first concerns and questions. In October 2008, the American Academy of Pediatrics began recommending that all children be screened for signs of autism at 18–24 months during their routine "well baby" checks (Martin 2010). If your doctor does not do a developmental screening test at your child's checkup, ask that it be done. The Modified Checklist for Autism in Toddlers or M-CHAT is a screening instrument that should be available to doctors.

Autism can sometimes be detected in children 18 months of age or younger. By age two, the diagnosis can be made reliably by an experienced professional:

Although research has revealed that autism can be diagnosed accurately as young as twenty-four months, the average age at which children receive a definitive diagnosis of autism is still three to three-and-a-half years. (Stone and DiGeronimo 2006, p.28)

As emotionally difficult as it is to pursue answers by seeking a diagnosis for a very young child, it is important to do so. One of the few facts we are sure of about autism spectrum disorders is that the earlier a child is diagnosed and receiving interventions, the better the long-term prognosis. It used to be the norm for physicians to want to watch and wait for young children to catch up or develop skills. With the benefits of early intervention, we now know it is important not to wait.

Some parents may be concerned about having a "label" for the child. Family members may be so frightened by the idea that something is wrong that they may try to keep a parent from getting a diagnosis. They may feel that if you don't name it, maybe it isn't real. Some may fear that once the child is diagnosed their educational and future employment records will be tainted for life. This will not happen and avoiding a diagnosis doesn't change how your child is perceived by others (Martin 2010).

In addition to being the "ticket" your child needs to be able to access crucial interventions, having a diagnosis helps you understand your child. It provides a context for the child's differences and needs. It gives you a starting place to begin to learn more about how to help your child.

> When I learned in November that my three-year-old son Ethan had a diagnosis on the autism spectrum, I was delighted. An odd reaction, perhaps, but I hoped that a diagnosis meant answers. Since the spring, my husband and I had struggled to find a solution for Ethan's increasingly frustrating behavior. (Ariel and Naseef 2006, p.107)

The diagnosis can also help the family connect with the community for support and services and can provide them opportunities to meet others who know what they are going through. This helps families feel less alone.

The diagnostic evaluation should not take place during a brief visit to the child's doctor. Children are unpredictable and may have behaviors at the doctor's office that are unusual or they may not be able to do certain things "on demand" in the doctor's office that they can do at home. The doctor can't possibly have enough information in a brief visit to diagnose an autism spectrum disorder. After I first heard about the possibility of autism for my son, I took him to see his pediatrician. It was a big practice with multiple doctors and the doctor who saw him that day was not very familiar with my son. When I told him that the speech clinician had suggested autism, he looked at Eric and turned to me and said, "Look at him. He's talking. If he has autism, then I'm the Pope!"

The evaluation should be done by a professional trained in using the DSM-IV manual (described below) and preferably also experienced with autism spectrum disorders. It should be thorough and take several hours and should include interviews with the parents, observations of the child, standardized tests, and review of medical records and any previous reports. It is also helpful to include cognitive testing as part of the evaluation to determine the child's level of intellectual development. If your physician dismisses your concerns and tries to "diagnose" your child without adequate information, you need to be persistent and trust your instincts about your child. Remember, you know your child best.

Diagnostic and Statistical Manual

The *Diagnostic and Statistical Manual of Mental Disorders*, fourth edition, text revision (DSM-IV-TR), is published by the American Psychiatric Association (APA 2000) and is the resource used by physicians, psychologists and psychiatrists in diagnosing individuals. There are currently five pervasive developmental disorders (PDD) listed within this manual, better known as autism spectrum disorders. The ASDs range from the more severe form, autism, to a milder form, Asperger syndrome. If a child has symptoms of either of these disorders but doesn't meet *all* the criteria for either, the diagnosis will be pervasive developmental disorder—not otherwise specified, the third category of ASD.

The other two disorders currently included under the ASD umbrella are two rare disorders, Rett syndrome and childhood disintegrative disorder (CDD). Rett syndrome occurs almost exclusively in females and is characterized by autism-like symptoms appearing between six months and 18 months of age with a steady regression in mental and social development. It affects one out of 10,000 to 15,000 children. CDD is also a rare form of ASD and is almost exclusively found in boys. Regression usually begins between three and four years of age. Until this point the child's development is normal, with normal

31

communication and social skills until the regression begins. The regression is extensive, involving motor skills and language and is more dramatic than losses sometimes seen in autism (National Institute of Mental Health (NIMH) 2008).

It is important to note here that the DSM-IV is in the process of being revised and a fifth edition is set to be released in 2013, after the publication of this book. My understanding is that the general category will officially be changed to autism spectrum disorders and will no longer include separate diagnostic criteria for Asperger syndrome, PDD-NOS or childhood disintegrative disorder. Each will be subsumed into the category of "Autistic Disorder." For more information on the proposed revisions to the DSM-IV, you can visit www.dsm5.org/Pages/Default.aspx.

Personal characteristics and behaviors

You may be wondering how this connects to your particular loved one with autism spectrum disorder. How might ASD show itself in someone? Children on the autism spectrum usually don't look physically different from other children. The differences will typically be seen more in behaviors and how the child relates to others. All individuals diagnosed with an autism spectrum disorder have impairments in three areas: in social interaction, in verbal and non-verbal communication, and in repetitive behaviors and interests. In addition, most individuals with ASD also have unusual responses to sensory experiences (NIMH 2008).

It is beneficial to describe each of these areas and some characteristics or behaviors that you may see in your loved one with ASD. Please keep in mind that not every child will show all of these difficulties and the symptoms may appear differently in each child. If you were looking at a room full of children with ASD you would see some children sitting by themselves and some playing with others. You would see some children talking and some not talking. Some children would be behaving well and some would probably be in the midst of a tantrum. As you read the characteristics described below, also remember that symptoms can and often do improve over time.

Social interaction

In the area of social interaction, most children with ASD have great difficulty learning to interact with other people. They may have trouble learning to take turns and to share. Some children may want friends but don't understand how to develop friendships. For these reasons a child may not initiate social interactions or show interest in other children. "If your child does not have difficulty initiating or responding to interactions with others, then your child does not have autism" (Stone and DiGeronimo 2006, p.12). They may avoid eye contact or seem indifferent to other people or prefer to be alone. Not responding to their name being called is often one of the first symptoms that parents may see. They may not use non-verbal gestures such as waving or nodding their head. They may not smile in response to praise.

Children with ASD are typically slower to learn how to interpret what others are thinking and feeling because they have difficulty picking up on gestures, facial expressions or body language. They may not follow a point of another by looking in that direction. They often don't look at people's faces to seek information or to read their expressions to know what they are feeling.

Children with ASD often do not imitate the behavior of others— one way that neurotypical children often learn. They also have trouble seeing things from another person's perspective. They may have difficulty regulating their emotions and may appear immature or have inappropriate outbursts. They may seem to have no "filter" and may blurt things out or be brutally honest. Children with ASD may have a tendency to "lose control" and get very upset, especially in a new or overwhelming environment.

Verbal and non-verbal communication

In the area of communication, difficulties may present themselves in verbal or non-verbal ways of communicating. The ability to understand spoken language is often also impaired. Many children with ASD have difficulty understanding the process of communication at all; they may not know the function of communication as a way of conveying their needs to other people. They may have difficulty in asking for help or asking for more. They may not communicate to share their interests such as holding up an object to show someone or pointing to an object.

The way the child's language develops, or doesn't develop, is often the first sign parents see that something is different. It has been estimated that up to 25 percent of children with ASD do not talk at all (Connolly *et al.* 2011; Prescott 2011). Those children with autism spectrum disorder who remain non-verbal throughout their lives can learn to communicate using pictures or sign language. But many children with ASD have language. Some have a delay in developing language compared to what is typical. Some children have what is called "regressive autism" and will develop language at the typical age of 12–18 months and then lose the words they have. And some children with ASD are only mildly affected in the area of language and may have only slight delays.

Those children with ASD who speak may use language in unusual ways. They may speak with a very flat, robot-like voice. They may speak in single words or repeat phrases over and over. They may parrot what someone says, something called "echolalia." Immediate echolalia is when they repeat something that has just been said. Delayed echolalia is when the child repeats something they heard in the past. Perseverative echolalia is when a child repeats the same phrase over and over (Notbohm 2005). Children without ASD go through a stage using echolalia but it typically passes by the time they are around three years old (NIMH 2008). Some children with ASD may actually have very precocious language at a young age and use very adult-like vocabularies. Despite having what appears to be excellent language, they often struggle with having a reciprocal conversation with another person. They may be able to speak at length about their favorite subject, but may not allow anyone else to participate in the conversation.

Other symptoms of the autism spectrum disorder can affect the child's success with communication with others. They may not understand another person's body language or tone of voice. They may not understand sarcasm or certain phrases of speech and may tend to take what people say very literally. Because of the difficulty that children with ASD have with using gestures and facial expressions when they communicate with others, their expressions and gestures may not match what they are saying. Their tone of voice may not reflect what they are actually feeling.

If the child does not have meaningful language or gestures to ask for things, they may have difficulty getting what they need. They may scream for what they need or just grab what they want. This inability to communicate their needs can lead to a great deal of frustration for the child and can result in inappropriate behaviors. It is important for families to understand that many of the child's behaviors may be the child's efforts to communicate to others and express what they need. When the child develops better communication skills, oftentimes the behaviors will improve.

Repetitive behaviors and interests

The third area of impairment that we see in children with ASD is in the area of repetitive behaviors and interests. Your loved one with ASD may exhibit certain repetitive motor movements that seem to have no function. We refer to these movements as self-stimulating behavior or "stimming" and many experts believe they are a calming mechanism for the child (Tilton and Thompson 2004). They may be very noticeable or very subtle. Some of the more common self-stimulatory behaviors seen in individuals with ASD include: flapping of the hands or arms, rocking, walking on the toes, pacing back and forth, spinning the body or objects, opening and closing doors, repeatedly turning lights on and off, and repeating words or phrases over and over.

Self-stimulatory behaviors can draw attention to the individual with ASD when they are in public or around other people. They may make the child look odd and make them stand out from other children. This can lead to the child being "picked on" or teased by other children. The behaviors can also sometimes be fairly loud and may disturb other people around them. For these reasons, parents and family members are sometimes upset by these behaviors and would prefer they be stopped.

My son has always "stimmed" quite a bit and still does as an adult. I have discovered over the years that Eric feels a very strong need to do these behaviors. Often, when we try to extinguish these behaviors, they will come out in some form at another time. Trying to extinguish them completely may not be in the best interest of the individual. They may feel the need to do this and may be calmed or comforted by these behaviors. Some families learn ways to minimize the behaviors at certain times, like in school, church or other public environments, allowing the child to "stim" at scheduled times in specified places like at home or in the car.

The way a child with ASD plays with toys may look different from other children. They may not play with a variety of toys but instead always want to play with the same toy. They may focus on a part of the toy rather than the whole toy such as focusing on the wheels of a toy car and not playing with the whole car in a normal way. A child with ASD may not play with toys in the way they are designed to be used and may not have functional play with toy figures, dolls, etc. For this reason, looking at the play skills of a young child during an evaluation can give important information about the child.

Another repetitive behavior children with ASD may have is to line up toys or objects. If someone accidentally moves a toy from the line, the child may get very upset. Children with ASD often need order, consistency and predictability in their lives. I believe that my son with autism often felt that his life was out of control. His need for routines and consistency were his way of establishing some predictability in his life. Much like lining up objects and getting upset if the order is changed, any changes in routines around bedtime, eating, going to school, etc. would cause intense meltdowns or tantrums. It would take a very long time to calm Eric and these disruptions would be exhausting for everyone in the family. With reactions like this, you can understand why parents may try to limit changes and new experiences for their children with ASD.

Repetitive behaviors can also include intense preoccupations with things or topics. For example, a child may insist on always holding or carrying certain objects in their hands. They may insist on picking up any stick they see on a walk or pick at any string they see on someone's clothing. The child may have an "obsession" with certain topics such as fans, the weather, animals, Thomas the Tank Engine, vacuum cleaners, stop signs, train schedules, etc. Often we see children with ASD who have great interest in numbers or letters or science topics. These interests are more powerful than what you might find in a neurotypical child. The child with ASD may be so driven to talk or think about their interest that it interferes with any other activity, often consuming the life of the child and the family. Preoccupations with objects can also make transitioning from one activity to another very difficult, especially if the activity they are doing relates to the intense interest.

Before you go crazy with your child's current obsession, keep in mind that these preoccupations can change over time. Eric's big interest was letters and numbers early on, which was helpful for learning the skills he needed for school. He also had an intense interest in animals and we owned every book and video we could find about them. His interests expanded over the years to include dinosaurs, extraterrestrials, Big Foot, and the Loch Ness Monster. These intense interests are not always a bad thing. They can be helpful in providing motivators for teaching the child new things and new behaviors. Some of these interests can be developed to become possible job skills for the future. Eric now works in a veterinary school at a large university and is surrounded by other people who love animals. His interest in animals helped to open doors to new opportunities.

Sensory issues

Many individuals with ASD have sensory issues and may have unusual reactions to the way things sound, smell, taste, look or feel. These reactions may be extreme and very obvious or can be subtle. Heightened sensitivities to sounds and touch can actually cause pain to the individual with ASD. Sometimes the feel of a certain texture of clothing on their skin can be unbearable. Noises that we may not even hear may cause intense pain to those with ASD.

> Usually, these sensory difficulties aren't due to any physical problems with the eyes, ears, mouth, or nose; they occur at the level where the brain processes input. So the body may collect sensory information properly, but the brain doesn't interpret the information properly. (Shore and Rastelli 2006, p.23)

Parents often have to act as detectives to determine if their child is bothered by the sensory stimuli in the environment. If children cover their ears often or avoid loud crowded situations, they may have heightened sensitivities to sounds. If they take their clothes off all the time, or complain about wearing certain items, maybe they are sensitive to the feel of the fabric on their skins. Some children may feel actual physical discomfort when someone hugs them and that is why they always pull away. A good rule of thumb is to think about the sensory stimuli in the environment when evaluating any behavior you may be seeing.

The visual sense may be a child's strongest sense and many students with ASD rely heavily on visual input to learn. However, this can be the first sense to become overstimulated and cause distress. Such things as bright lights, reflective surfaces and fast moving objects can be overwhelming to someone with ASD (Notbohm 2005).

> I think in pictures. Words are like a second language to me. I translate both spoken and written words into full-color movies, complete with sound, which run like a VCR tape in my head. When somebody speaks to me, his words are instantly translated into pictures. Language-based thinkers often find this phenomenon difficult to understand. (Grandin 1995, p.19)

The auditory sense is often impaired in children with ASD. Hyper-acute hearing can cause agonizing pain and sudden loud sounds can make the child panic. The child with ASD may have the inability to filter out everyday sounds that we tolerate with no problem, such as the dishwasher, the coffeemaker, the vacuum cleaner, etc. Many students with auditory sensitivities may have difficulty focusing on the voice of the teacher because of all the other sounds going on in and outside of the classroom that they find distracting.

The impairments of the tactile senses may appear in different ways. The hypersensitivity to touch may make the child sensitive to even the lightest of touches from another person. However, some individuals with ASD crave a deep pressure kind of touch. Some children may have difficulty tolerating textures involved in certain play activities like handling play-doh or glue or sifting in a sand table. My son seemed to have a phobia about the feel of the slick pages in a magazine. He would not be able to sit anywhere near a magazine and definitely wasn't able to touch one. Luckily that sensitivity has improved and now, as an adult, he can tolerate the feel of the pages long enough to read an article he is very interested in, but he still won't leisurely thumb through a magazine for fun.

Sensitivities to textures and sensory issues around smells and taste can cause certain food preferences and intolerances. There are many children with ASD who are extremely picky eaters and may eat only a very few kinds of foods.

> When people hear about Jake's food issues, they roll their eyes. Many suggest that we just leave him at their house for the weekend. They figure we're not trying hard enough, or that we give in too easily. But they don't know Jake, whose anxiety about food is stronger than hunger. (Brodey 2007, p.18)

Other conditions

There are other conditions that can be involved in some individuals with ASD. A report published by the CDC shows that 30–51 percent (41% on average) of children who had ASD also had an intellectual disability (CDC 2010a). One in four children with ASD develops a seizure disorder (NIMH 2008). Hyperlexia, the ability to read very early, is often associated with ASD. Other conditions such as obsessive compulsive disorder and attention deficit/hyperactivity disorder are also seen quite often in individuals with autism spectrum disorders.

If you are reading about these symptoms and characteristics of ASD and have not already pursued an evaluation for your loved one, you should contact your child's doctor and share your concerns. The doctor should be able to refer you to a specialist who is knowledgeable about autism spectrum disorders and can do a thorough assessment. Developmental pediatricians, child neurologists, and child psychologists or psychiatrists are professionals you may consider contacting for an evaluation.

In the United States, you can also call your state's public early education system to request a free evaluation to see if your child qualifies for intervention services. If your child is under three years old, you would contact your local early intervention system. Early intervention (EI) services are available in the United States for every child from birth to three years of age. Your pediatrician should be able to give you more information about EI services in your community. Or for a listing of EI programs by state, you can go to the National Dissemination Center for Children with Disabilities (NICHCY) website at www.nichcy.org/Pages/StateSpecificInfo.aspx. If your child is three years old or older, you should contact your public school system. The same website listed above will give a list by states of the programs for children with disabilities between the ages of three and five. As I said before, an early diagnosis and intervention services can be crucial for the best prognosis for the child.

TREATMENTS

As I stated earlier, currently there is no cure for autism spectrum disorders. There are, however, many types of treatments or therapies that can help. Children with ASD can improve and they often do. Certain interventions may benefit your loved one more than others. It depends on the child and their individual strengths and needs. "Finding the right intervention program begins with an understanding of your child's learning style" (Stone and DiGeronimo 2006, p.102). Once you understand your child's learning style, you may find that one sole treatment will not satisfy what your child needs and that a combination of different treatments may be the best option for your child.

The cost of treatment also plays an important role in what interventions a family may choose for the child. It is very expensive to care for a child with an autism spectrum disorder. According to a study done at Harvard University in 2007, the cost of raising a child with autism over their lifespan can add up to $3.2 million per person, as compared to the $222,360 it typically takes to raise a child to age 18 (Ganz 2007). Obviously, a family's financial situation can directly influence what treatment options they will pursue. The costs of many treatments can run between $30,000 and $100,000 a year (Shore and Rastelli 2006).

Before I describe some of the more popular therapies and interventions, I would like to give you some advice. First of all, be careful of what you read on the internet. I often think that my life would have been much easier if the internet had been available when I first learned about my son's autism. I was so desperate for information. As I am writing this, I did an internet search for autism spectrum disorders and got over 2,750,000 hits! The problem with the internet is that there is too much information and not all of it is reliable. "A large amount of what you can read about on the Web focuses on raising your level of paranoia about everything" (Siegel 2008, p.101). The best advice may be the simplest: if something seems too good to be true, it probably is.

I would suggest that you first ask your doctor about possible treatment options available in your community and see what he or she recommends. If you get connected with other family members of children with autism, I would ask them about their experiences with treatment options. (Keep in mind that all children with ASD are different and what works well for one child may not for another.) Then do your homework. Research the intervention you are considering and get as much information as you can. Take notes. It is difficult to retain everything you are learning. Find out where the treatment is available, how much it costs, how intrusive it may be for the child and the family, who provides the treatment, and if they are reputable.

You will also want to find out if the intervention has been validated scientifically. I know this sounds like a lot of work but these may be some of the most important decisions you ever make, for your child and for the rest of the family. If you are overwhelmed by taking care of your child and family, ask someone to help you with this. This would be a great task for a friend or extended family member to do for you.

All the early interventions my husband and I received for my son were chosen with the following criteria in mind: the cost, the distance from our home, whether it could be worked into our family schedule, and whether Eric could tolerate it. We relied on other parents of children with special needs and the professionals who were helping Eric to advise us about what strategies might help. When we considered new therapies we often had to rely on our instincts about whether the intervention was legitimate and would help Eric.

When your child is evaluated and receives a diagnosis, you should also receive information from the evaluator about your child's strengths and challenges. This information will help you better understand your child's needs and how to address them. The evaluator should also be able to offer advice about interventions and direct you to some possible resources in your community.

There are many educational and treatment approaches available. Keep in mind that you don't necessarily need to choose only one strategy to help your child. Many families find that treatments can be used together and can reinforce each other. They are not mutually exclusive. Sometimes a combination of several different approaches helps the child the most.

Speech, language, occupational, and other therapies

There are several interventions that are often provided free of charge through school districts or regional service organizations. Speech and language therapy (SLT) is typically needed for children with autism spectrum disorders and can help improve the child's communication skills. It can be administered individually or in a group. Occupational therapy (OT) teaches skills that help a person live as independently as possible. For the child with ASD it may focus on building skills used in getting dressed, eating and bathing, and fine motor skills needed in school. Some OT therapists are also trained to do sensory integration therapy, another form of intervention that may help a child deal with sensory information. Physical therapy (PT) is another therapy that may be offered through your school district. It can benefit those who have low muscle tone and delays in gross motor skills (CDC 2010c). Physical therapy can help build strength, coordination, and basic sports skills (Rudy 2011). Although many school districts offer these services free of charge, some parents may choose to supplement the school therapies with therapy from private practices in the community.

Speech therapy and occupational therapy may be included in the early intervention services in your community. As I mentioned before, early intervention is considered a treatment that can greatly improve a child's development. EI services help children from birth to three years old learn important skills including how to talk, walk, and interact with others (CDC 2010c).

Children who are enrolled in early intervention services will have a plan outlining the services they will be receiving, called the individualized family service plan (IFSP). It is a whole-family plan in which parents are major contributors. Other team members can include medical professionals, child development specialists, therapists, and social workers. The types of services that may be included in the plan in addition to speech and occupational therapy are family training, physical therapy, psychological services, transportation, nutrition services, assistive technology and service coordination (Martin 2010). Service coordination can be especially helpful to a family just learning about their child's needs and the resources that may be available to help the child. Remember, even if your loved one has not yet been diagnosed with ASD, he or she may be eligible for early intervention treatment services.

Applied behavioral analysis

Applied behavioral analysis (ABA) is the oldest and most fully researched treatment specifically developed for autism (Rudy 2011). It is a reward-based therapy focused on teaching particular skills. Many schools and treatment clinics use ABA. It encourages positive behaviors and discourages negative behaviors while improving a variety of skills. There are different types of ABA including discrete trial training (DTT), pivotal response training (PRT), and verbal behavior intervention (VBA) (CDC 2010c).

Developmental interventions

"Floortime" is a developmental intervention for children with ASD. Its official name is developmental, individual differences, relationship-based approach (DIR). This intervention focuses on the emotional and relational development of the child and is based on engaging the child in play initiated by the child. Another developmental therapy is relationship development intervention (RDI). Developmental therapies typically build on a child's own interests, strengths and developmental level to increase emotional, social and intellectual abilities (Rudy 2011).

Visual strategies

The Treatment and Education of Autistic and related Communication-handicapped CHildren (TEACCH) program is another intervention specifically developed for individuals with ASD. TEACCH uses visual strategies to teach skills. Visual strategies may provide the structure and predictability needed by many children with ASD. The consistency that visual strategies give may make the child feel safe and help with transitioning and allow more flexibility. The "structured teaching" methods of the TEACCH program help make the environment more predictable and understandable for the individual with ASD.

Another intervention is the Picture Exchange Communication System (PECS), which is a communication system that uses picture symbols to teach communication skills. The individual with ASD is taught to use picture cards to request what they need and to communicate their feelings.

Other interventions

The Social Communication, Emotional Regulation, and Transactional Support (SCERTS) model was developed by Barry Prizant and four other experts in the field of autism and is similar to the TEACCH model. SCERTS is more of a philosophy than an intervention. It begins with the assessment of the needs of the child before determining what interventions will best fit their needs. The child is considered an active participant in his or her learning and heavy emphasis is placed on the coordination of all persons who are involved with supporting the child (Shore and Rastelli 2006).

Medications

Medications are another treatment that can be helpful to some individuals with ASD. There are currently no medications that can cure ASD, but there are medications that can possibly improve some of the symptoms. For example, there are medications that can help manage anxiety, energy levels, depression or seizures. There are also medications to help treat severe behavior issues such as aggression or self-injury. Again, you should consult your child's physician before considering any medication treatment. The National Institute of Mental Health autism website has more information about medications at www.nimh.nih.gov/health/publications/autism/complete-index. shtml#pub4 (CDC 2010c).

Diet

There are also dietary approaches available that may be helpful to in-dividuals with ASD. A popular dietary intervention used with children with ASD is the gluten-free and casein-free diet (GF-CF diet). It is based on the belief that autism is caused by a poorly functioning gas-trointestinal system and that removal of gluten and casein from the diet will improve symptoms of autism. Gluten is a protein found in products containing wheat, oats, barley and rye. Casein is a protein found in cow's milk and other dairy products. Many diet treatments have not been validated scientifically so families need to be careful in pursuing these interventions. You can always find anecdotal stories from parents who feel a diet is helping their child but remember that what seems to work for one child, may not for another. You should always consult your child's doctor or a nutritionist before engaging in any change in diet or introduction of any vitamin or mineral supplements.

Alternative treatments

Sometimes families choose treatments that may be controversial or not typically recommended by physicians or professionals. These treatments are known as complementary and alternative treatments and include the dietary supplements and special diets that I described above. Chelation or heavy metal detoxification is another therapy that is considered an alternative treatment. It involves drugs administered to remove the heavy metals from the body and is based on the belief that autism is caused by abnormally high levels of mercury that accumulate in body tissues (Stone and DiGeronimo 2006).

"Current research shows that as many as one third of parents of children with an ASD may have tried complementary or alternative medicine treatments, and up to 10% may be using a potentially dangerous treatment" (Levy 2003, p.418). Biomedical treatments are also considered a complementary and alternative treatment. Many are based on the Defeat Autism Now! (DAN!) protocol. DAN doctors may prescribe special diets, supplements, and alternative treatments. Although the US Food and Drug Administration and CDC have not approved these treatments, there are many stories of positive improvement (Rudy 2011).

Researching interventions

This list of some possible treatments for ASD may leave you feeling more confused than ever and I apologize if all this information is overwhelming to you. I have tried to highlight just a few of the interventions and give you a basic description. You will need to research them more thoroughly. The book *Understanding Autism for Dummies* (2006) by Stephen Shore and Linda Rastelli has a very complete listing and description of many treatments and might help answer questions you might have. *Does My Child Have Autism? A Parent's Guide to Early Detection and Intervention in Autism Spectrum Disorders* by Wendy Stone and Theresa DiGeronimo (2006) is another resource that may be helpful to you as you research interventions.

PROGNOSIS

The prognosis or potential for a child with ASD is as difficult to predict as it is for neurotypically developing children. We could never predict what our neurotypical children will be like as adults so how could we do that with our children who have ASD? Some children are severely affected as a young child but make incredible gains. Some very mildly affected children when young are more affected and limited in adolescence and adulthood. It's impossible to predict accurately what the future will hold. But parents and family members almost always have questions about their child's future, especially immediately following getting the diagnosis. I remember asking the developmental pediatrician who diagnosed my son about his future; what he would be like when he is an adult, will he get married, and will he be able to take care of himself. She had probably answered these kinds of questions many times before. She informed me that she didn't know what the future would hold. She reminded me of all the strengths he had, that he was very young, and there was lots of time to help him learn and improve. Whatever the diagnosis may be, whatever the child's current challenges, he or she *will* make progress and will continue to learn throughout their lives.

MYTHS

You now have more information about what ASD is and how it may appear in your loved one. ASDs are becoming much better known due to frequent coverage by news media and the increase in characters with

ASD in TV shows and movies. Despite all the information out there and the publicity this condition receives, there continue to be misunderstandings or "myths" about ASD that some people still believe. The following are some of the current myths you may have heard.

Everyone with ASD has extraordinary "savant" abilities

The reality is that relatively few people with ASD are savants like the character Raymond in the movie *Rain Man* (1988). Some may have what are called "splinter skills" of special ability, such as incredible skills in math, in memorizing facts, etc. but this is definitely not seen in the majority of individuals with ASD. The other myth related to this one is that everyone with ASD has an intellectual disability. This is also not true. Intellectual ability varies across the spectrum of autism.

People with ASD don't have feelings and do not show emotion

It is not true that individuals with autism cannot feel or express love or empathy. They may simply lack the skills to communicate their feelings. Most individuals on the autism spectrum are capable of expressing many feelings, however sometimes it may not be seen in the "typical" ways. Individuals with ASD may need some help in identifying their emotions and learning the correct way to show them, but they definitely have feelings just like all of us.

People with ASD can't build relationships with others

Although it may be a challenge for many individuals with ASD to initiate conversation and participate in social situations, most develop strong relationships with others. Close relationships with family members and friendships with other individuals who share similar interests are very possible. There are also many adults with ASD who get married and have very satisfying romantic relationships.

Individuals with ASD are
not able to communicate

We know there are individuals with autism who are non-verbal or nearly non-verbal, but that does not mean they are not able to communicate. There are many ways to get your needs across to others including sign language, gestures, or using a picture form of communication. We also know that there are many individuals with ASD who are extremely verbal and are very capable of communicating with others.

Early intervention is the only key to
improvement in children with ASD

We know that getting treatment when a child with ASD is young is very important to their future. But the years before the age of five are not the only time when interventions can make a difference. Learning doesn't stop at age five. Children with ASD are continually learning and there is no time limit on building skills for the future.

Children with ASD need to go away
to "special autism schools"

Many educational options exist today for children with ASD. All children within the public school setting in the United States are entitled to an individualized educational plan (IEP). As part of this plan, a team, including the parents, will decide on the best supports and resources to help the child be successful. The type of classroom and level of supports will depend on the needs of the individual child. It may be determined that the best setting is a class specifically for students with special needs. Or the best setting may be total inclusion in a regular education classroom. Or the child may need some combination of each of these options. Some children do go to private schools, some are home schooled, and some go to specialized schools for students with autism. But there are many options available.

Individuals with ASD
cannot be successful as adults

There are many self-advocates, or individuals with an autism spectrum disorder, who are successful in their lives and who have been able to share their experiences and knowledge with the world. Temple Grandin is probably one of the most famous adults with autism. She has written many books about autism and gives presentations around the world. There is a popular movie about her amazing life and success as a highly educated professor and animal facilities designer. There are also those who don't reach the same level of education and notoriety as Dr. Grandin but who are successful as well. Adults with autism can be very hard workers and make excellent employees. They can be creative thinkers and innovators and add a unique perspective to the world. Individuals with ASD, with the support of their family, friends and community, can lead full lives and contribute to society no matter what their level of challenges.

Chapter 2

LIVING WITH ASD

A family's life changes dramatically when a child is diagnosed with an autism spectrum disorder. Each family's experience will be unique because every child with ASD will have their own unique challenges and strengths. But there are commonalities in the experience. This chapter focuses on how the diagnosis can change the daily life of the family. It also describes the variety of emotions that parents find themselves balancing during the early days after the child is diagnosed.

If you are a parent of a newly diagnosed child with ASD, you may be reading this to learn more about what to expect as you start on this journey. You may want to know how your personal experiences compare to what other families are going through. Whatever you are going through, please know that you are not alone. I hope that the comments and experiences of other parents included in this chapter will validate your own feelings and experiences.

For extended family members and friends, understanding what the family may be going through is an important step to being able to support them. Even if you have a close relationship with a parent of someone with ASD, they may not be sharing what they are going through with you. You may not be spending enough time with them or the child to understand the impact ASD may be having on the family. The information in this chapter should help you understand more about the day-to-day challenges of raising a child with ASD.

Most people will never fully comprehend what living with ASD is like if they don't have a child with the disorder. No matter how much information the parents may share about their life and their child, no matter how much the family members and friends learn about the disorder, it is impossible to understand all the challenges the family may be facing. But it doesn't matter if others fully understand; just the attempt to understand can mean a great deal to families.

> I remember crying when I told my parents and siblings. It actually took me years to be able to tell people without getting emotional… They were all understanding, loving and very supportive. The funny thing is, all these years later (almost 15) I still think that only a small part of my family totally understands what our day-to-day life can be like. (Parent of E)

The beginning of this experience is probably the most difficult time. Adjusting to this new life can be very stressful for parents. Sharpley, Bitsika, and Efremidis (1997) reported in the mid-1990s that the three most stressful factors for parents of children with ASD were: the permanency of the condition, the lack of acceptance of the behaviors associated with ASD by family members and society, and the low levels of support that are typically provided (Sharpley et al. 1997). There isn't anything currently that can be done about the permanency of the condition. That will always be a stressful factor for parents. But there are many interventions that can improve the symptoms and behaviors and let's hope that as society is learning more about ASD, there will be more acceptance and more support for families.

CHANGES FOR PARENTS

After receiving the diagnosis of an autism spectrum disorder for their child, parents are often in shock. They may have suspected something was wrong, but they probably never expected it to be ASD. Of course nothing has actually changed with their child. He or she is still the same child the family loved before receiving the diagnosis. But everything feels like it has changed as the parents try to cope with the news and adjust their lives accordingly.

There was a feeling of everything being out of control. This "thing" had invaded our lives and taken over. I couldn't make it go away. I couldn't even understand it. My beautiful little boy had not changed, but in reality everything had changed. The way I looked at him and talked to him changed. The way I thought about myself had changed. My life, Eric's life, and my family's life had changed and I had no control over it. (Morrell and Palmer 2006, p.17)

The only real change is that now the parents have a diagnosis that can help them understand and treat the child's behaviors. Getting the diagnosis is crucial for helping the child, but parents may find it hard to see anything but the diagnosis.

Parents have said it feels as if their child has been kidnapped by an ASD in the middle of the night. The picture of the child is replaced with a picture of an ASD. The diagnosis of an ASD becomes the newest member of the family. (Exkorn 2005, p.250)

Parents' views of themselves can also change after receiving a diagnosis for their child. Consider what Robert LeVine said about the typical goals of parents when they have a child. He explained that all parents share common goals: to protect their children, to nurture their children so that they reach adulthood successfully, and to have a rewarding personal relationship with their children (LeVine 1988). Getting the diagnosis of ASD threatens parents in all three of these basic parenting goals. Parents may already feel they have failed in protecting their child; they could not protect them from the diagnosis. They aren't sure what their child's future will be and probably question whether they will be able to parent or nurture their child to adulthood successfully. And having a rewarding personal relationship can be challenging with a child who struggles with social interactions.

Helen Featherstone in her book *A Difference in the Family: Life with a Disabled Child* (1980) describes how parents of children with disabilities may view themselves.

> Suppose I, an ordinary person, am walking alone beside an icy isolated river and see someone drowning. I have two options: I can jump in and try to save him (risking death myself), or I can agonize on the shore. In the first case I am a hero; in the second a coward. There is no way I can remain what I was before—an ordinary person. As the mother of a profoundly retarded child, I felt I was in the same position: I had to look like a hero or a coward, even though actually I was still an ordinary person. (Featherstone 1980, pp.83–84)

Parents are still "ordinary" parents despite the new information they have received about their child. But parents may feel that they must now be extraordinary parents in order to help their child. At the same time that parents are putting pressure on themselves to be superparents, the diagnosis can be a blow to each parent's self-confidence and self-esteem. There is a mystery surrounding everything about the child and what the parent should do. The parent doesn't know what caused this. They don't understand their child's behavior. They are unprepared for all the things they must do to take care of their child. The parent is suddenly an educational advocate for their child, a position they never thought they would be in and one they are poorly prepared for. And the parent has no idea what to expect for their child's future. It's no wonder parents don't feel confident in their role as a "more than ordinary" parent.

Even if the parent has some knowledge about ASD or experience with special needs children, they may still feel blindsided by the diagnosis.

> A decade ago, I had graduated from a university with a degree in psychology—I had even written my thesis on autism! And yet I had given birth to and lived with a child for four years and

not even recognized he was on the autism spectrum. (Ariel and Naseef 2006)

The parents' daily life also changes dramatically after receiving the diagnosis. They may be driving their child to numerous doctor's appointments, special schools, and therapies. Parents are entering a system within the schools that they never thought they would need and working with people they never thought they would meet. They may be making drastic changes to their child's diet which can change how they prepare food for the entire family. They may be starting an intensive home therapy for their child and thus disrupting their normal family routine. Parents may become so busy with the care of the child with ASD that they can't maintain the friendships they had before the diagnosis. Oftentimes parents end up making changes within themselves to match the changes in their new environment. Their priorities, beliefs, attitudes, values, and daily routines may undergo major changes.

The ASD diagnosis is also going to affect the family's finances. Parents may have to adjust their work schedule in order to take care of their child. Parents of a child with autism are three times more likely to have to quit their jobs or reduce their working hours than parents of children with other chronic health issues. They pay more on average for their child's healthcare and therapies and spend more time providing or arranging for that care (Mozes 2008). With the added financial pressures, a parent may have to take on additional jobs to help cover the expenses of raising a child with ASD.

Parents are likely to be physically and emotionally exhausted during the early years. If they have a child who doesn't sleep well, parents may also be sleep deprived. Lack of sleep drains a person's energy and affects their ability to cope. It can rob them of perspective and the capacity to concentrate and solve problems. By increasing levels of the stress hormone cortisol, sleep deprivation wreaks havoc with parents' emotions. It can make them feel irritable, angry, and depressed. It's no wonder sleep deprivation is used in psychological warfare as an effective form of torture (Morrell and Palmer 2006).

Many children with ASD are very active and parents may become physically exhausted from chasing after a hyperactive child all day long.

> We are always tired from chasing G around the house trying to avert disasters. My house is always a mess; I don't even let anyone ever come over because I am too embarrassed about the way it looks. We are just too tired to do anything about it. (Myers, Mackintosh and Goin-Kochel 2009, p.676)

Many children with ASD are in constant motion and may not be aware of danger. They may have incredible climbing skills and want to repeatedly climb to the top of a bookcase or the refrigerator and jump off. They may be impulsive and have no fear of cars and suddenly dart out into traffic. They may try to eat or drink things that are dangerous. Parents who are dealing with these kinds of issues must be constantly "on alert." This can be physically exhausting as well.

> I could never, ever, let my guard down, and by the end of the day, the strain of always trying to stay one step ahead of his overactive mind exhausted me physically and mentally. (Brodey 2007, p.64)

> He has given my life so much happiness, because I love him no matter what's wrong. But also he has given me so much fear. He has no sense of danger, and I'm terrified he'll run in the road or get lost. I am the only one that really can give all the energy and patience it takes to take care of him. I am exhausted. (Myers et al. 2009, p.673)

Many parents choose to ignore their own physical and emotional needs and spend all their energies focusing on the child's needs. Although well intentioned, this can lead to physical and emotional burnout for the parent. It is important for parents to take care of themselves so they remain healthy and can physically handle the needs of the child and the family. Also, if the parents are emotionally exhausted and not thinking clearly, they can't be a good advocate for their child.

> Sleep deprivation and emotional exhaustion interfered with my ability to concentrate. I left many meetings not totally understanding or remembering what was discussed or decided. (Morrell and Palmer 2006, p.83)

RESPITE CARE

Many families turn to respite care to relieve the physical and emotional exhaustion they may be experiencing. In the world of special needs, respite care is a support that provides temporary care for children and adults with disabilities. It can be a life-saver for some families who desperately need a break from the daily stresses of taking care of a child with ASD. Respite care can be as simple as having someone come into the home while the parent is there, allowing the parent to get a shower, do the laundry or take a nap. It can involve having someone come in the home for a few hours so the parents can go out. The individuals providing the respite for a family are often paid professionals but they can also be family members or friends who are volunteering to help.

There are also respite services available in many communities where you can leave the child or adult for an hour or two at a supervised program. Some respite programs even provide caretaking training for parents and family members so they can learn more techniques to care for their loved one (Exkorn 2005). Parents should look into what is available in their community.

When my children were young, my husband and I were often overwhelmed with the challenges of taking care of Eric's needs and the needs of our other two children. We arranged a weekly "date night" and had someone come to the house to babysit the children so we could go out for a few hours. Most of the time the grandparents helped with the babysitting but occasionally we used a teenager in the neighborhood or professional respite providers from a local organization that worked with individuals with disabilities. We had to force ourselves sometimes not to cancel our scheduled date night when we were tired. It was important for us to give ourselves these evenings alone to be a couple and not talk about the kids or the "A" word (autism).

We were very fortunate to have people available to us to provide our much needed respite. We were also fortunate that Eric's behaviors and needs at that time were not overly challenging and we felt comfortable leaving him with other people. Some parents may hesitate to make use of respite opportunities. They may believe they are the only ones who are able to take care of the child adequately.

> Someone suggested getting out on our own to avoid depression. But how can we do that, when we are like glasses/hearing aids/leg braces/tour guides for our children? How could I just take away the tools he needs to live? (Brodey 2007, p.34)

Parents may not want to use respite support because the child has challenging behaviors or requires complicated routines that parents consider too difficult to explain to someone else. Some children with ASD can't tolerate strangers coming into their home and disrupting their routines. It is understandable that leaving the child with others may just be too anxiety-provoking for some parents. There are many reasons why it may not be easy to use respite, but there are also many reasons why taking a break is important for the physical and emotional well-being of the parents.

PARENT EMOTIONS

Parents of children with ASD are also going to be impacted emotionally from this experience. They typically find themselves trying to balance many different emotions, especially right after receiving a diagnosis for their child. Parents are sad about the loss of the child they thought they had. They are worried and fearful about the unknown future for their child. Parents may feel overwhelmed with all they need to learn and understand to help their child. They are most likely confused by the conflicting information they are receiving and confused by their child's behaviors. They are frustrated because they can't fix what's wrong with their child and improvements are not happening fast enough.

It's important to note that parents' feelings following the diagnosis are very complicated. How they feel about their child's differences is influenced by their beliefs and attitudes about disabilities, their spiritual beliefs, and their expectations about parenting. The feelings parents have are also going to change over time and from moment to moment (Whiteman and Roan-Yager 2007). The most important thing to remember is that there are no right or wrong feelings. Every parent will respond to this experience in their own way. It is important to understand that these feelings are a normal part of the adjustment to living with ASD.

Sadness and grief

Sadness may be one of the first emotions that parents are confronted with when their child receives the diagnosis of ASD. Every parent has expectations of who their child will be. When a child is diagnosed, they may be feeling a loss of the dream life they expected for their child.

With the confirmation of our worst fears, I felt lost and inconsolably sad. I had expected a child with unlimited potential, a Justin who would be the perfect combination of all of our best qualities. (Morrell and Palmer 2006, p.23)

Parents may also feel the loss of the life they had expected for themselves. Having a child with ASD can mean giving up employment opportunities. Due to the cost of medical care and treatment for the child, the parents may have a different financial situation than they expected. Their leisure activities may also be impacted by having a child with ASD. They may not be able to travel or go on the vacations they would have planned if they hadn't had a child with ASD. Their social opportunities may change because they are overwhelmed with the care of their child and have little time to maintain friendships.

Grief is an appropriate response to loss. It's what you feel when something or someone you love is taken away (Martin 2010). A diagnosis of autism or ASD feels like something has been taken away. Sometimes others may not understand this level of grief because there is no actual death of a child. But feeling grief from this experience is normal and expected, and each parent will go through this process in their own way.

I remember a physical pain. It's hard to describe but I felt it deep inside of me. I cried for several days, performing all the necessary tasks like taking care of my children, eating, bathing, etc., but I walked around like a zombie. (Morrell and Palmer 2006, p.16)

Researchers often describe grief as a progression from one stage to the next, moving to a final stage of acceptance. My experience of grief was much less orderly. I felt like an all-news radio station: all emotion, all the time. Overwhelmed by the enormity of Justin's needs, I alternated between paralysis and hyperactivity. (Morrell and Palmer 2006, p.25)

For the initial days after the diagnosis, people seemed to know that I needed some "isolation" to think and process. I did end up reaching out when I needed, but I definitely needed those first few days to process the grief. My husband and I cried together and processed together, and that was really all I needed or wanted of any family member or friend initially. After that, it didn't take me long to reach out to extended family and friends. (Mother of A)

Sadness and grief not only are present during the time immediately following the diagnosis, but also can last for a long time for some parents. The parent should talk to their physician if the sadness persists and impacts their ability to function. The comments below are from a parent who was suffering from depression and struggled to make the decision to contact her doctor.

> I started to entertain the notion that if I were dead, I could at least get a decent nap... I struggled *a lot* with the decision to call my doctor. It felt tantamount to admitting defeat. I felt like I was admitting that I didn't have faith in my son's ability to grow up to be a functional member of society, and that I didn't have faith in my ability as a parent. (Brodey 2007, p.65)

For many parents the sadness dissipates over time and becomes less overwhelming in their daily lives. However, sadness can emerge again off and on over the years at unexpected times—at birthdays and family events, and at times of expected milestones for the child that are not met. Again, this is normal and is part of the adjustment process.

The grieving process and adjusting to the diagnosis is very individual and will look different for every parent. Some parents will have difficulty grieving. They may equate it with weakness or a loss of emotional control (Marshak and Prezant 2007). They may feel that experiencing grief means the parent doesn't love their child or that they have given up on their child.

Some parents experience grief but don't allow themselves to show those feelings in order to protect their partner.

> I wasn't brought up to have feelings. My father never showed his feelings. He was always strong. I thought I had to be strong too, especially in front of my wife. I felt like I had to protect her. But one day I just couldn't hold it in any longer. I went into the bathroom and started to cry. I guess Kathy heard me because she came in. I don't think she had ever seen me cry before. But she put her arms around me and held me... She said afterwards she'd been waiting for me to do that! (Simons 1987, p.26)

Although some fathers may fear that breaking down in front of their wives will add to their pain, most wives don't agree and want their husbands to show what they are truly feeling. "I hated it when he bottled it up inside. I knew he was miserable but he didn't want me to see. That just made me feel like I had to hide my feelings" (Simons 1987, p.27).

Denial

Denial is sometimes a byproduct of grief. It is essentially a defense mechanism that people use to protect themselves. It helps parents temporarily protect themselves from things they aren't able to handle until they are more able to manage the truth. A parent in denial may not believe the diagnosis or may blame other reasons for the child's unusual behaviors.

My husband was in denial for years and still is to some extent. He did not want our son to get therapy of any kind. I had to do it behind his back at first and he never went to meetings with doctors or the school. (Autism Speaks 2009, p.6)

When the speech clinician mentioned possible autism, I could not see the autism in my son. I could find a logical reason for everything that was different about Eric. I went to the public library and looked at what few books there were about autism and none of the case studies I could find described a child like mine. Our friends and family members also couldn't believe it could be autism. Everyone had a story of someone they knew who didn't do this by then, or did something weird as a child but eventually grew out of it. (Morrell and Palmer 2006, p.16)

A father commenting on the fact that he kept lists of things his son could do to challenge the diagnosis: "I think I was trying to prove to myself, it was futile in hindsight; I was trying to prove to myself and the world that Maxwell was not autistic" (Schall 2000, p.411).

Sometimes a parent may see no reason for concern at all, and think the child is just fine. This example of denial is more likely in families where the ASD characteristics are very subtle. The parent may say, "He's just a boy," or "She'll grow out of it." What is especially difficult is when one parent is in denial about the diagnosis and the other parent isn't, which can cause major conflicts for the couple. Another form of denial can be when a parent agrees with the diagnosis but believes that if they just do enough treatments, it will make their child "normal." Mounting a "crusade" to defeat the ASD can cause added stress on the family.

Unfortunately, it is next to impossible to make someone accept the truth when they are not ready. It's important to remember that denial is a way of coping. People don't consciously choose this reaction, it just happens. Gently talking about it or gradually giving pieces of information that supports the diagnosis might help. The passage of time may also help as more information is understood and more time is spent understanding the child's differences.

Hope

Sadness and hope go hand-in-hand for the parents of a child with ASD. Parents may be very involved and invested in helping their child improve and at the same time struggling with feelings of loss. This ambiguity and the highs and lows that go with it can require a great deal of energy from parents (O'Brien and Daggett 2006).

Parents of children with disabilities often speak at one moment about their depression and despair, and in the next moment talk about how wonderful their child is. In case studies done by Larson in the late 1990s, six mothers of children with disabilities reported that they felt grief and joy, hope and fear, acceptance and despair. All of them wished for miraculous cures and wanted their children to be "normal" but at the same time they spoke of their love for their children just the way they are (Larson 1998).

Sometimes professionals working with a family may think that parents' hopes are unrealistic. With their knowledge of ASD they may feel that the parents' expectations for the child are too high. And in fact the parents' hopes may be unrealistic. But hope is necessary to help the parents cope and survive the challenges they are facing. It is that hope that drives the parents to do everything they can for their child. This quote from a father of an eight-year-old son with autism helps explain the importance of hope for parents.

> Imagine for a moment, how even more daunting your family's battle with autism would be without hope. Without hope, you would not hire therapists. Without hope, you would not enlist the help of friends and family. Without hope, you would not dare to dream. Without hope, autism wins and your child loses. (Ariel and Naseef 2006, p.83)

Feeling inadequate

It's understandable that parents may feel inadequate for the task they have been given. They have the overwhelming responsibility for educating themselves about ASD. They have to make important decisions about which treatments or interventions to try. They must pick knowledgeable caregivers and therapists to work with their child. They have the responsibility of choosing the schools and programs that will be most beneficial to their child. And on top of all this, they must be the case manager for all their child's healthcare needs (Shore and Rastelli 2006). It's understandable that parents may not feel adequate for the job.

Parents often feel inadequate in their role as a parent, especially if they are a first-time, less-experienced parent. This parent of a three-year-old with autism writes about her disappointments in herself: "I broke all the rules today: The 'Be Consistent' rule. The 'Never Give In' rule. And especially the 'Always Be Patient' rule" (Brodey 2007, p.76). Parents may set the bar too high for themselves and have difficulty meeting those expectations.

Unfortunately, we live in a world preoccupied with perfection. When parents are raising a child with ASD, they realize that they are imperfect parents and also parents of imperfect children—a double blow in the perfection-preoccupied world! So it is understandable that parents may put pressure on themselves to be the perfect parent. But raising a child with ASD challenges all of a parent's skills and being a perfect parent is impossible. Parents do not have the training to raise children with ASD when their child is diagnosed. They are presented with the situation and learn to cope, adapt, and do the best they can.

Confusion

Most parents feel confused after receiving the diagnosis for their child. They may question if the diagnosis itself is correct. It is a complicated diagnosis and not easily understood. Parents are probably receiving too much confusing information to digest. Professionals and family members may be confusing them further by giving conflicting advice. It's hard to know who to believe.

> One of the things I found to be especially frustrating was the lack of communication among the different agencies or programs that were working with my child. Each program was giving us different advice and strategies to help Eric, with little consideration of what another program might be doing. As a parent new to this and not confident at all in my knowledge of autism and the decisions I was making for my child, it only deepened my feelings of inadequacy. (Morrell and Palmer 2006, p.133)

Following the diagnosis, a parent is trying to learn to be an "expert" about their child. But at the same time, the parent is suddenly *expected* to be an expert on their child and a strong advocate for them. They are doing all this while trying to balance the needs of their family and their own needs as a parent.

> When Justin was first diagnosed I found that the advice meant to encourage me actually had the opposite effect. Professionals and older parents reminded me that I was the expert on my child. I knew this was meant to make me feel included as a

valuable member of the treatment team. But the thought that I was the expert on Justin only added to my already sizable panic. If I was the expert, then we were in much deeper trouble than I had originally believed. (Morrell and Palmer 2006, p.134)

Feeling overwhelmed

During the time immediately after receiving a diagnosis for their child, most parents feel overwhelmed. There is just too much to do and too little time in the day. Parents want so much to help their child in every way possible that they can easily overextend themselves. I like this parent's strategy to confront feeling overwhelmed.

Sometimes things get overwhelming. Sometimes I cry simply because there is too much to do or remember. But I find myself to be a better parent if I do not get caught up in how much there is to do but rather look at how much I have accomplished today. (Marshak and Prezant 2007, p.137)

The expression "take one day at a time" is very appropriate for parents in this situation. Thinking about the future is overwhelming. Focusing on today is manageable. With everything they are dealing with each day, parents must recognize that they can't do it all. They can then decide which things are most important to do, which things they can delegate to someone else, and which things are just not important enough to do at all. Parents often get caught up in the drive to "fix" their child and end up trying to do too much.

I was guilty of this myself. Following Eric's diagnosis at age two, I had him enrolled in two preschools, a "typical" preschool and a speech and language preschool. I took him to private occupational therapy once a week and private speech therapy once a week. I took him to the TEACCH Center once a week. I also took him to our local elementary school once a week for OT and speech therapy offered by the public school. And on top of all this, I was trying to work with him individually every day. I was doing all this while also parenting a six-week-old baby! I felt like we were living in our car. Although I was definitely overextended and overwhelmed, Eric's therapies in part were my "therapy" too. When I did all these things, I felt a little more in control during a time when everything felt totally out of control.

Not only are parents feeling overwhelmed with everything they have to do for their child, they also feel overwhelmed by the amount of information they must process. They are researching strategies and therapies and trying to become better educated about ASD and about their child. They are getting information from the schools, doctors, therapists and the media. Many parents discover that their brains can only process so much information before going into overload. Once they are in overload, they stop processing and stop understanding.

Parents can regulate how they manage information overload by setting the pace with which they are expected to absorb it. One solution is to break down information into manageable chunks. Parents can tell those giving them information that they need time to process what they are being told. Parents can also try to go together to meetings or ask a friend or family member to attend a meeting so there will be more than one person hearing the information and less chance of confusion later (Marshak and Prezant 2007).

Fear

Another very strong emotion parents are feeling following the diagnosis is fear. Parents are afraid for the future because they don't know what it will hold for their child. They are afraid for their child; will they be accepted or rejected? Will they be bullied or taken advantage of? Parents are fearful of the responsibilities they will have. Do I have what it takes to be a good parent for my child? Can I take care of my child and do everything I need to do to help them?

Fear was the most difficult emotional companion in my early life with Justin. I felt haunted by an endless cycle of unanswerable questions, especially at night. Would we be able to provide for Justin and his many needs? Would our marriage make it through the struggles and challenges of this difficult child?

> Did we have the capacity as individuals and as a couple to love him when he could act so unlovable? Would it be fair or humanly possible to raise other children in this environment? (Morrell and Palmer 2006, p.25)

That fear sometimes drives families to take extreme measures to keep their children safe.

> I feel really bad about this, but we have to lock him in his room at night. It is the only way to keep him safe. Otherwise, he might come downstairs and try to cook something, or start a fire in the fireplace or worse leave the house and wander away or something. (Schall 2000, p.413)

Fear can make parents feel very protective of their children. Parents feel that something bad has already happened to their child (the diagnosis) and want to work diligently to keep anything else bad from happening to them. The "mama or papa bear mode" may come out at times when the parents feel their child is in danger or at risk. Other people may not understand this behavior and may think that parents are being overly protective. But parents know their children, and they know how vulnerable they can be. They have probably seen bad things happen and their protectiveness is only to prevent those situations from happening again. The fear that parents feel is what drives them to keep their children safe.

Anger

Sometimes parents are going to feel anger, at the disorder, at God, or at life in general. Why me? Why my child? What did we do to deserve this? Parents may feel angry at those who give the diagnosis or those who point out what they don't want to face. They may also become angry when they don't feel they are being supported; when friends or family don't make contact or show support. Or they may get angry when the system is not responsive and the services and supports they need aren't available. The anger is a reaction to the pain they are feeling and the target of that anger may not always be logical. Unfortunately, anger can be difficult for family members and friends to accept and tolerate. Parents who are angry at others may be rejected by the people who could be the most supportive to them.

Loneliness and isolation

Families with a child with ASD often become isolated from others and understandably feel lonely. The parents may not have the time to contact friends or family for support.

> I had a great group of friends before my daughter's birth. But the birth of my daughter with autism seemed to close down my community. I was so focused on her therapies and care that I lost touch with many people. (Parent of C)

It is too difficult sometimes for parents to go out into public if they have a child who has unpredictable or odd behaviors. The negative reactions from strangers can be very painful. The thought of dealing with the stares or comments from strangers in the mall or the grocery store may be too much for some parents and they may find themselves rarely leaving home. "We pretty much stay at home; there is no eating out at restaurants, no family vacations, very few family outings" (Myers *et al.* 2009, p.680).

> It was hardest when I would have no idea why my son was upset. From Eric's point of view, something wasn't happening as it should have, and I often had no idea what it was or how to fix it. In order to avoid the stress of these difficult behaviors our family lost all spontaneity. Before we did anything or went anywhere we had to ask ourselves how Eric would react. New situations were avoided if at all possible, and because outings into the community could be so difficult, we found ourselves staying home more and more. (Morrell and Palmer 2006, pp.18–19)

My husband, my older son and I never do anything together. One of us (my husband or I) stays home with our son with autism—we do not travel as a family; we do not celebrate holidays with extended family, etc. (Myers *et al.* 2009, p.680)

We became more homebound because it was just easier. New places were always hard and big groups were difficult. We did a lot of "one parent" events. One of us would take the other children and the other would stay home with our youngest (with autism). Usually I was the one that would stay home. (Parent of B)

Just having a child with a complicated, lifelong disorder is isolating as it is. It changes your life and can make it very different from the lives of your neighbors and friends. Parents may have difficulty finding things they have in common with their friends or neighbors. And when your child's disability is invisible to others, which it often is with ASD, it can complicate your relationships even more. People who don't understand autism, who don't *see* anything different physically with the child, may assume the child is just acting-out or the parent is overreacting. When the parent is already feeling inadequate and is questioning their parenting skills with this complicated child, being judged by others may just be too much to deal with.

People have steadily helped me into isolation. Family, friends, spouse, the person in front of you at the grocery store—they'll tell you he behaves like he does because you are too strict, too lax, too distant, too pampering. They aren't trying to be cruel; they want to help... And you believe them, because you wish it were true. If his behavior were your fault, then you could work to change it. (Brodey 2007, p.35)

Guilt

With the current emphasis on the prevention of disabilities, it is not surprising that parents may struggle with feelings that they may have inadvertently caused their child's autism. There is no definitive cause of ASD at the present time. This gives room for parents to blame themselves. Although we know autism is not caused by poor parenting, parents might still feel guilty about why this happened. They may worry about something they did or didn't do during the pregnancy. They may feel guilty about passing down the autism genetically. I have met parents who feel that they deserved this somehow because they aren't a good enough person or didn't have enough faith in God.

Parents may feel guilty about other things apart from the cause of the autism. They may feel guilty about not realizing something was wrong earlier and waiting too late to start treatments for their child. They may feel guilty about the choices they are making or not making for their child. Sometimes parents will feel guilty when they get angry at their child or are embarrassed by their child.

But when you love someone, you expect yourself to love to be with them. When you don't feel that and think you should, the guilt can be unbearable. (Ariel and Naseef 2006, p.252)

Frustration

Parents are also going to feel frustrated. Although they may be getting multiple therapies or interventions for their child, progress may be slow.

As a special-needs kid, you have twenty failures for every success. With "normal" kids, you may experience twenty successes—spontaneous kisses, or lessons grasped—for every failure. (Brodey 2007, p.34)

It is frustrating for parents to try so hard to help their child and not see improvement immediately.

Parents may also feel frustrated when they can't understand their child. When parents can't determine their child's needs, both the parent and the child are left feeling frustrated. The child's behaviors are often totally unpredictable and parents find themselves frequently trying to figure out what happened and why. I remember a ferry ride our family took in Delaware when Eric was young. For some reason when the ferry started leaving the dock, Eric became hysterical. Something was wrong and I had no clue what it was. He screamed at the top of his lungs repeatedly, "Start over! Start over!" Obviously we couldn't get the ferry boat captain to start the trip over so we had to watch him sobbing for the entire trip and try to console him the best we could. We never did figure out why things didn't go as Eric expected and why he was so upset. We always felt like detectives trying to figure out our child.

It can also be very frustrating when others don't understand. Friends and relatives may not understand the complexities and the difficulties the parents are facing daily. Strangers may not understand autism and may say or do things that are hurtful.

Acceptance

Despite some of the stresses and difficult emotions parents go through that I've described in this chapter, life does improve. Parents of newly diagnosed children, who are in the middle of that overwhelming and scary time of adjustment, need to hear that it will get better. Children with ASD are always learning and will develop in ways that we may not expect. Dealing with the really difficult times gets easier, not necessarily because the situations are easier, but because with time we as parents become stronger. The experiences we live through and the things we learn from our children over the years gives us more confidence in our abilities to make the right decisions. We continue to have situations that scare and overwhelm us and we may always fear for our children's futures. But there are always strategies to try and people to go to and lean on (Morrell and Palmer 2006).

Once parents and others who care about the child with ASD reach a point of acceptance of their life and acceptance of their child for who they are, things get easier.

> Somewhere along the line, life stopped feeling like a tragedy and just became what it was. Living with unpredictability became the only predictable pattern of our lives. Balance and humor returned; regrets and comparisons faded… It amazes me that, on many days, the pleasure of having Justin in my life now outweighs the pain. It's not that living with Justin became easy—it did not. It's not that pain and sadness did not recur—they did (and still do). But as Justin began to learn and mature, he developed some mastery over his life. And as I began to learn and mature, I developed some mastery over mine. (Morrell and Palmer 2006, pp.28–29)

Over the years, I've spent a lot of time grieving for what I thought were losses in Eric's life when in fact he was very happy and didn't seem to miss what I thought he was missing. I remember taking him to birthday parties for children in his preschool class. I was so excited that he was invited and would finally maybe make some new friends. I would watch him at the party. He would go off by himself and play alone. He didn't watch the other children or care about what they were doing. He didn't eat the food the other kids were eating. When they sang "Happy Birthday," Eric would cover his ears. I would cry while driving home from the party, sad about everything Eric didn't have in his life. It finally occurred to me that Eric didn't like going to these parties. He was miserable. I was trying to get him to like things that were important to me, that reminded me of what a "normal" life should include. I began to stop feeling so sad about how different his life is from what I expected and to be happy that Eric is happy, that he has a full life, and that he is loved by many people.

Reaching that point of acceptance is not an easy journey and is something all parents have to go through in their own way. Parents' definition of acceptance can change and mean something one day and something totally different another. Parents may feel very accepting of their child and their life, and then the next day they may feel overwhelmingly sad about something missing from their life. Maybe the point of acceptance for parents is simply the time they reach in their lives when the good feelings they have about their child occur more often than the bad feelings. The autism becomes only a part of their lives, one of many complications and features, and not the driving force.

POSITIVES OF THE EXPERIENCE

Despite some of the difficult aspects of living with autism that I have described, there are many positives in this experience. The changes that come into your life are not all negative. Autism may bring some incredible people into your life. Chances are you will have a better appreciation of what is important in life and what isn't. You may become more patient and more understanding and accepting of the differences in others. Caring for your child or loved one with ASD may give a special meaning to your life. In the quotes below, parents describe what this experience has meant to them.

> The good things have been that we have had to work together for our child, make long term plans and set goals, have more of a tolerance for problems in general, have a stronger faith, and we've had to depend on one another. (Brower and Wright 1986, p.11)

> I thought I could change him and make him the boy I wanted him to be, frantically and persistently following various treatment approaches... Despite intensive treatment, he did not make dramatic progress. Instead he has been a catalyst to transform me, and help me to become the man I needed to be. He taught me the meaning of unconditional love—to honor his sacred right to be loved for who he is, not what he has achieved lately, how he looks or how much money he will earn. Without words, he continues to teach me a priceless lesson. (Ariel and Naseef 2006, p.250)

I've been completely humbled by a disorder that is incomprehensible. I've been humbled by the inner strength my husband possesses, the tenderness of my children, the support of my parents, but mostly by the profound love I have for them all. There is empowerment in that kind of love. (Ariel and Naseef 2006, p.27)

Justin also helped me redefine what constitutes a quality life. Justin is deeply loved by his family. He lives in a place where people strive to understand, encourage and care for him. He works where he is expected to contribute, but is not judged by his productivity. His life is filled with many activities that he finds pleasurable. From the time of his childhood when I despaired that he would ever be happy, it is now more surprising to see him upset. Justin helped me to see that my vision of what constitutes a quality life was too narrow. Given his significant limitations, I really believe the quality of Justin's life is remarkable. (Morrell and Palmer 2006, p.175)

I worry less now. I know not to take anything for granted. Perhaps that's one of the blessings wrapped up in the sometimes difficult world of autism. We parents know how to celebrate the good times, and we also know they don't always last. [This experience] has taught me not to judge and to go with the ebb and flow of my son's sense of himself and the world as he experiences it. It has shown me that he is much more than a child on the spectrum of autism. He is a whole human being whose wiring and inner world are unique to him—an extraordinary person in an ordinary world. (Sell 2007, p.200)

The pain I felt when Eric was first diagnosed is hard to remember now. That deep feeling of loss is not there anymore. How can having Eric in my life be a loss? Loving him has enriched my life in many ways. He is constantly teaching me new ways to look at things. His brutal honesty and innocence reminds me of how superficial people can be, and what is important in life (and what isn't). He has taught me to judge people less and accept people more. I have a much deeper appreciation of all people who are different, not only people with disabilities, but people who make different life choices or have different beliefs from my own. (Morrell and Palmer 2006, p.186)

Her illness is not a gift, but *she* is a gift. I will always be grateful that we have ended up in this life together. (Whiteman and Roan-Yager 2007, p.178)

Chapter 3

MOTHERS, FATHERS, AND SIBLINGS

In the previous chapter we discussed the changes that take place for parents following the diagnosis of a child with ASD. We also talked about the different emotions the parents may be feeling. This chapter focuses on how living with ASD impacts individual family members and their relationships with each other. Mothers and fathers may have very different responses to the diagnosis. How each of them copes with this experience can affect their relationship as a couple. Siblings of the child with ASD may understand and respond to the diagnosis differently, and this will influence the relationship they have with their brother or sister with ASD throughout their lives.

MOTHERS

In most families mothers are the primary caregivers for the children. Though there are many families where both parents work outside the home, the nature of the challenges of ASD can often require one parent to stay home to care for the child. That parent is most often the mother. Researchers at the University of Pennsylvania have found that mothers of children with ASD were 5 percent less likely to have a job than the mothers of children who have other chronic health problems. They were 12 percent less likely to have jobs than mothers of children without disabilities or health issues. The study also found that mothers working outside the home are taking lower-paying, more flexible jobs so that they can spend more time taking care of their autistic children.

This occurs more often in families with children with ASD than in families with children with other health problems (Reinberg 2011).

The mother is typically responsible for the daily care of the child as well as the majority of transportation to therapies, doctor appointments, and schools. After the child receives the diagnosis, the mother is usually responsible for setting up therapies at home, researching the resources available in the community, observing schools and classrooms in order to find the best placement for the child, etc. Mothers in essence become case managers for their children with ASD and must balance that role with the daily responsibilities of taking care of the family.

Mothers, in particular, have been found to have poorer mental health, poorer physical health, and lower quality of life when they are parenting a child with ASD as compared with mothers raising neurotypically developing children or children with other disabilities (Myers *et al.* 2009). Mothers of children with ASD typically report higher levels of parenting stress and depression than the fathers (Davis and Carter 2008; Hastings *et al.* 2005). These studies remind us of the importance of support for mothers of children with ASD.

As mentioned above, mothers have traditionally been the primary caregivers and are largely responsible for the health and welfare of their children. They take these responsibilities very seriously. When their caregiving abilities are challenged by autism, mothers may blame themselves if their child has difficult behaviors or doesn't reach milestones when expected. The stares and comments from strangers may feel like a criticism of the mother's ability to parent their child. Having a child who is a picky eater or a child who isn't potty trained can feel like a personal failure to the mother. In general, many mothers of children with ASD doubt their abilities to be a "good enough" parent. This may be why so many mothers try to cope with the situation by immersing themselves in advocating for their child.

> I have mastered the role of being Sara's advocate. I believe this is inexplicitly entwined with the responsibility of being her mother. (Sell 2007, p.229)

An advocate is defined as a supporter or defender; someone who speaks, pleads or argues for someone or something. As an advocate for their child with ASD, mothers and fathers must speak up for their child within the school system and medical health community. They also must educate others about their child, whether they are teachers, professionals or people in the community. Although both parents must be advocates for their child, it is often the mother who is the first line of defense, the so-called "frontline advocate" for their child with ASD.

This job as advocate is a new experience for most mothers and can be quite overwhelming. The quiet, shy, authority-respecting woman may need to become the aggressive, demanding mother bear, fighting for what her child needs. This can be very uncomfortable for some mothers.

> The more information I amassed about this disorder, the more I began to realize that it was going to be up to me to make things happen—not only to find the best doctors, but to find a way to get on their busy calendars; not only to find the best school, but to get my son enrolled; not only to understand what the best intervention and treatment options were, but to make them a reality for Marty. (Martin 2010, p.16)

I remember feeling like I had to go into "pre-battle" mode before individualized educational plan meetings for my son, collecting all the ammunition I would need and developing a battle plan. As uncomfortable as it was initially, it became more comfortable over time as I got used to standing up for my child to school principals and teachers. Some mothers will adjust to this new role easily, while some will need time to learn how to be the best advocate they can for their child.

Advocating for a child with ASD is an extensive subject that will not be discussed at length in this book. There are wonderful books available for parents and family to help answer advocacy related questions. I highly recommend Areva Martin's book *The Everyday Advocate: Standing Up for Your Child with Autism or Other Special Needs* (2010). As a parent of a child with ASD and a lawyer, she has a wonderful perspective to share on this topic. For extended family members and friends the most important thing for you to know is how stressful advocacy can be for the parents. You can help the parents by supporting their decisions, helping them research their options, attending meetings with them if needed, and most importantly, by reminding them of how well they are doing advocating for their child.

For some mothers, focusing all their energy on helping the child can distract them from the stress and pain they may be feeling following the diagnosis. Working with the child makes mothers feel more capable as a parent and more in control of their lives at a time when everything seems out of control. The frustration of not being able to fix their child's problems is alleviated somewhat when mothers concentrate on their child's therapy and working with the child. This can become a problem, however, if the mother becomes too involved in working with the child and neglects taking care of herself and the other responsibilities in her life.

> A friend, who was also a special education teacher, offered a suggestion that led to one of the most important epiphanies in my life. She said, "You spend an enormous amount of your time, energy and money on treatment and education for Justin. Maybe as his mom you should try to enjoy him more and work with him less." (Morrell and Palmer 2006, p.140)

Mothers may also find themselves always looking for the ASD or thinking about the diagnosis every time they look at their child. It may be difficult to separate the ASD and see the child for who they are. Once they learn to let go of constantly thinking about ASD and worrying about the child's prognosis they will be able to see what is wonderful and special about their child.

Once I stopped being on high alert for atypical behaviors, I started noticing how my son looks out for the younger kids at the playground, the patience he shows with his senile great-grandparents, and how he saves even the smallest spider from being stepped on. I realized that he has the biggest heart of any person I've ever met. (Sell 2007, p.45)

Mothers typically have more opportunities than fathers to access support. They have more opportunities to meet other parents of children with ASD when dropping off their child at school or while waiting for therapy appointments. Also, support groups for mothers are often conveniently offered by schools and autism programs during the child's therapy or school time. Mothers are also typically more willing to open up to family members and friends about what they are going through and more willing to accept support from others.

FATHERS

Fathering a child with ASD has its own added stressors and the father's reactions to the diagnosis and parenting experience may be different from that of the mother. As mentioned earlier, women are often the primary caregivers of the child with ASD. As such, they often get a continual flow of information about the child's progress from doctors, therapists, teachers, and others. For this reason, women are often forced to recognize the reality of their child's disability. Fathers may not be receiving that same flow of information that can help them understand their child (Simons 1987).

The father's job can make it difficult to have the frequent contact with therapists and the school that the mother may have. By being less involved in the daily interaction with their child with ASD, fathers may have a longer period of denial about the disability and its implications. I often hear from mothers that the father does not agree with the diagnosis and thinks nothing is wrong. It could be that the father has not had the same opportunities to learn about how ASD affects their child. And sometimes what appears as denial may actually be just a different way of looking at things. A father of a son with Asperger syndrome explains:

> I think men get a bad reputation for not accepting disabilities. We may respond differently, but every father I have spoken to knows his child has issues. We are just as hurt and traumatized by the knowledge when we learn about it, but are expected to take strong roles and not react strongly. Part of this is to keep balance, I think. I have always accepted my son's diagnosis; I recognize he has problems, but in my eyes he is not disabled. He is, I think, "differently-abled" and needs help relating that to the real world. (Marshak and Prezant 2007, p.42)

Fathers may need more time to come to terms with the diagnosis and to get to know the child in their own way (Rudy 2009a). As we know, trying to interact with a child with ASD is not always easy and fathers may become frustrated. Mothers feel this frustration as well, but have more time in the day to practice strategies and get to know what works best with the child. Mothers also may have more opportunities than fathers to receive guidance from therapists and teachers.

Fathers may have more limited time to interact with the child. Most fathers come home after work in the evening when the family is getting ready for dinner and beginning bedtime routines. This is often an especially stressful time for the family when everyone is tired and patience is stretched thin. Fathers may have to work hard to build that close, interactive relationship with the child. Once they know how to relate better with the child, they often feel more connected.

Learning how to understand and interact with their child with ASD is essential for the father's relationship with the child. Jamie Winter, a research scientist at the University of Washington Autism Center, suggests that it is very important for both the child's mother and father to be involved in parent training whenever possible. Potential benefits from father participation include increased frequency of interaction and quality of interaction between fathers and their child with autism, increased treatment time for the child, and support for the child's mother (University of Florida Health Science Center 2005).

In Chapter 1 we discussed how isolated parents can feel when their child is diagnosed with ASD. Fathers often find themselves even more isolated than mothers. Dr. Vicki Turbiville, the project director at the Beach Center on Families and Disability, states that "systems, interventions and support are all built on 'mother models.' Many service providers want to deal with moms, not dads; they can't or won't schedule appointments and meetings at times when fathers can attend" (Rackley 2011, p.1). Professionals may automatically focus on the mothers when giving information and providing instructions.

> When the physician walked in to deliver the message he looked squarely in my wife's eyes. Even though we were sitting side by side, his eyes never made contact with mine... The physician...no doubt recognized the pain in my beautiful wife's eyes. The fact remained however, that I, the father, was also in a state of complete emotional collapse. The failure of this particular physician to even make eye contact with me seemed to send the message that...I was not hurting. (Rackley 2011, p.1)

Understandably, fathers may be feeling left out. It can help if mothers take the time to share the information they are getting from the professionals with the father. The mothers can also request that meetings be scheduled at a time when the father can attend. Understanding that the father may be feeling isolated, mothers can also encourage the father to participate more in activities with the child.

I realized that my husband was not having the opportunity to hear the encouraging words from the teacher when I would pick up Eric from school. He wasn't at the occupational therapist's office watching Eric work hard and hearing the therapist's praises. As a way to help him feel more connected, I would arrange home "work" sessions with my son when my husband would be there to watch and participate. He needed to see what goals we were working on and see Eric's improvements. He needed to feel like he was a member of the team helping his son and I needed his involvement with me.

If a mother wants the father to be more involved, it is important to be honest and suggest what might be needed and talk about ways the father can help. When the father does pitch in and help, the mother needs to appreciate his help and accept his way of doing things. Sometimes the mother may not want to share responsibilities with the father because he doesn't do things the way she prefers. The way a mother and a father interact with their child will be different and that is good for the child. We should recognize and value the differences between what fathers and mothers bring to the parenting experience.

When the kids were young I would occasionally go out of town for a weekend with other mothers of children with ASD for a much needed weekend away from autism and motherhood. I was thrilled that my husband was so understanding and supportive and was willing to take care of the kids while I was gone. Following one of these weekends I asked my daughter how things went during their time with Daddy. She reported that everything went fine but Daddy always fed them in shifts. Being able to simultaneously prepare multiple meals for three picky eaters was not my husband's strong suit apparently, but that was okay. I was just glad that everyone got fed and everyone was happy.

Women are often encouraged to express their emotions and to talk to others about what they are feeling. Fathers are typically not encouraged to express their emotions. Fathers of children with ASD are probably feeling all of the emotions mothers are feeling but are holding them inside. Some men consider their feelings as weaknesses and don't want others to see them. Some fathers may be holding in their emotions to protect their spouse from seeing how much they are hurting.

Fathers of children with ASD may be feeling powerless to protect their family from the autism. They may be frustrated that they can't simply work harder or pay more to fix their child's disability. Fathers, like mothers, have dreams for their child's life that may be threatened;

educational, athletic, vocational dreams, etc. They are grieving as much as the mothers but have fewer outlets to express what they are feeling.

> My wife's irrepressible optimism was a great asset from the outset. She devoured the autism literature and focused quite sensibly on what we could do to help Katie. She pointed out that my moping and feeling depressed wouldn't help Katie and make her autism go away. I pointed out that grief isn't something you can turn off at will. (Ariel and Naseef 2006, p.30)

Fathers of children with special needs may have very few support opportunities in their environment. If it requires added work to find these opportunities, fathers are going to be less likely to pursue them. But they too need to have a place to work through their grief, anger, and depression.

> Women report that their husbands usually did not or could not ask for support. They were less likely to express their emotions regarding how the family member with disabilities affected them. In many cases, husbands put themselves in a position where they pretty much said to their wives, "What do you want me to do (for you)?" Thus implying that they did not need any help themselves. (Brower and Wright 1986, p.18)

Unfortunately, the workplace typically doesn't offer the needed encouragement or support opportunity for fathers of children with disabilities. Most men find it awkward to share personal information with their co-workers. Family support groups in the autism community can be a possible option for support for fathers. There they can meet other families with similar experiences. Many fathers find these groups very helpful. Some fathers find support through making friends with another couple who have a child with ASD. In a smaller informal group the fathers can share experiences and be supportive to each other. This more intimate setting may be easier for some fathers who may be overwhelmed by the larger support group environments.

It is clear that fathers play a very important role in their child's life, especially in the life of a child with a disability. Although some fathers may distance themselves from the situation, most fathers will be understanding and active participants in raising the child with ASD. They, like mothers, will need support and encouragement from family members and friends to cope with this challenging experience.

THE RELATIONSHIP BETWEEN MOTHER AND FATHER

There is limited published information about the impact of raising a child with ASD on a couple's relationship. Some researchers have found that having a child with a disability has a negative impact and some researchers have found no differences between families with and without a child with a disability (Meadan, Halle, and Ebata 2010). Other researchers found that when marriages didn't survive, they broke down for several reasons: one parent was left doing most of the childcare and parenting, the parents couldn't agree on the diagnosis, parenting strategies or the child's needs, and the marriage was already weak to begin with (Baskin and Fawcett 2006).

For a relationship that is fragile or unstable, a disability can be "the last straw." On the other hand, challenging life events can serve as catalysts for change. Some families disintegrate while others thrive despite their hardships. People can emerge from a crisis revitalized and enriched. Hope for relationships really can spring from the crises people experience when their child has a disability. (Ariel and Naseef 2003, p.1)

Having two boys with autism was never in my thoughts before becoming a parent, but it sure has taught me about

unconditional love, and it has made my marriage stronger than
any marriage I know. (Myers *et al.* 2009, p.678)

Our instincts tell us that if a relationship is strong enough before
the diagnosis, chances are it will be strong enough to withstand the
stresses of autism. The same would be true for relationships that can
withstand job losses, a death in the family, financial difficulties, or
taking care of aging parents. Parenting a child with autism, like all
of these unexpected challenges, requires couples to work at keeping
their relationship healthy (Morrell and Palmer 2006).

Most of the time we felt like no one else understood what
we were going through. We felt like all we had to depend on
was each other. It made us even closer because we made our
marriage top priority. We knew it wouldn't do our son any good
to lose the security of both parents. We decided not to let ASD
be all our family was about. (Autism Speaks 2009, p.7)

Living with autism is a family matter and as such affects the rhythm
and the functioning of the whole family. That includes the marriage
or relationship between the parents. Every relationship is unique
but having a child with ASD creates predictable problems: coping
with a child with high needs reduces the time a couple can devote to
each other, and a couple's relationship is complicated by the strong
emotions that go with raising a child with a disability.

Overall, you can think of having a child with a disability as
amplifying what occurs in a more typical family and marriage.
Closeness may be stronger, divisions greater, anger intensified,
sadness deeper, parenting decisions weightier, and happy
times more exhilarating. (Marshak and Prezant 2007, p.viii)

How the parents react to the diagnosis can be a source of stress on
a relationship. We often expect our partner to respond the same way

we do but men and women typically respond differently to problems and show different emotions. The grieving process is going to look different for each parent. The diagnosis is a subject that is often hard to talk about. Parents may be feeling too much pain, blame, anger or guilt to put their feelings easily into words. Both partners may be too afraid of hurting the other. Sometimes these strong emotions and how the parent reacts to them can be misunderstood.

A father confided that he was struggling with feelings of anger and grief about his young son's autism. He felt unable to share these feelings with his wife, because he knew how upset she was over their son's diagnosis. As her husband, he believed he needed to be strong and protect her from his sorrow. Ironically, a few weeks before, his wife had shared how upset she was by her husband's lack of distress about their son. She could not understand why he did not seem to care very much about the boy's problems. She felt all alone with her sadness. (Harris and Glasberg 2003, p.88)

There are ways parents can manage their different reactions to grief. To keep connected, parents should keep their communications open and rely on each other for support. They need to make time for each other whenever possible and share in the decision making and activities concerning the child with ASD. Attending the child's therapies together can keep parents on the same page about the child's progress. No matter what the differences are in the reactions to the diagnosis, it is important to give each other time through this process and if things don't improve, seek help professionally (Baskin and Fawcett 2006).

Experiencing the stages of grief differently isn't always a bad thing. Sometimes parents balance each other. The partner who is feeling more optimistic provides support and encouragement to the one that is feeling depressed. Or the parent who is ready to give up can be refueled by the energy of the other parent (Whiteman and Roan-Yager 2007).

He's always been a quiet support. He is becoming more verbal and an active contributor through the years. We seem to have a scale we keep in balance—when he is down I am up and vice-versa. (Brower and Wright 1986, p.12)

I would say that husbands and wives need to give each other the freedom to cope with and express feelings differently. My style of coping is to gather as much information as I can about the disability and treatment. At first, when my husband didn't behave the same way, I thought he didn't care. Now I realize his focus is more on how our son is like other children. I think this gives our son a healthy balance. (Marshak and Prezant 2007, p.30)

The search for information and treatments for the child can bond a couple, but if one parent is doing all the work and the other is in denial or distant, that can cause problems as well. I often see mothers putting all of their energy into helping the child and the father feeling left out. If one parent puts all their energy into the child, there is simply no energy left for the marriage.

It is typical for the role of mother and father to take precedent over the roles of husband and wife, especially when the child is young and the needs are great. The mother may be exhausted and dissatisfied if the father is not available and the father may be exhausted from added work responsibilities and dissatisfied with the attention he gets at home. Both may feel unsupported by the other (O'Brien and Daggett 2006).

My husband is very supportive of me and works hard to provide for me and our children. However, it is a challenge to share intimate moments. I think he doesn't think that he is a priority for me. (Autism Speaks 2009, p.5)

> The roles and responsibilities of being a father and a husband often get intertwined… Overcompensating in one role usually means you're neglecting the other role. For a long time I didn't get it when my wife criticized me as a spouse. After all, I was doing more for our son than almost any father I knew. Eventually, I understood that I was doing a great job meeting my son's needs but not hers. One does not make up for the other. (Marshak and Prezant 2007, p.xxi)

The relationship between the mother and father can also be affected by the stress of choosing the best services or therapies for the child. Choosing interventions is very complicated and involves investigating all the different options, finding providers of the intervention, possibly fighting with insurance companies for coverage, and physically getting the child to appointments. All of these activities can be stressful on a couple and can present opportunities for disagreement.

It is important to remember that it is a lengthy adjustment process for a couple dealing with a diagnosis of ASD for their child. Whatever the experience a couple is having, it takes time to adjust and cope as this parent describes:

> When we first realized there were problems with our son, we both dealt with it differently. We eventually felt a real strain in our marriage; we had some long talks (late at night) and slowly started working together. It took about three years to fully accept our son's special needs. Since that acceptance, our relationship has grown stronger. (Marshak and Prezant 2007, p.36)

Knowing that having a child with ASD adds stress to a marriage, there are things that can be done to help the relationship before there are problems.

Work to understand each other's needs

Be kind to each other in this difficult time, and consider each other's emotions and wants, as well as their needs. "No matter how long you have been married, you sometimes need to teach your partner what you need rather than get upset when he or she doesn't intuitively anticipate your needs" (Marshak and Prezant 2007).

Spend time alone together

Set aside time together alone. This may be difficult but it is important. A close bond between partners can help parents get through the rough spots.

It is almost as if we have two separate relationships. We have our relationship, our love affair. And then we have the relationship that we share as parents. We always agree in the love affair. (We usually don't agree in the parenting.) This has always kept us together at points when things got very tough. (Marshak and Prezant 2007, p.5)

My wife was always there to nurture or to help adjust my attitude. She is my best friend. (Brower and Wright 1986, p.12)

Take care of your individual selves

Don't forget to take care of yourself and add some fun into your life (alone and together).

Reach out

Share the responsibilities at home when possible. Work together to learn about your child's disability.

My wife was always positive and wanted to know what she could do to help. There was a time that the family responsibilities were taking over my job. My wife took the initiative to get the information we needed and brought me along. We learned together. (Brower and Wright 1986, p.12)

Become involved in a supportive community

Reaching out to your partner, relatives or friends can help lessen the burden. Meeting other parents of children with ASD can be helpful. Be open to receiving support.

Communicate

Resist the tendency to blame, and instead ask for what you need. Don't expect your partner to know how you feel and what you are thinking. Tell your partner what he or she is doing right. Work through the painful feelings and arrive at some form of joint acceptance and effective parenting strategies. Remember you are both on the same parenting team.

My husband always supported me the most by being open, willing, and demanding good communication. (Brower and Wright 1986, p.12)

Seek assistance if needed

It is not a sign of weakness to seek help when you need it. If it becomes hard to function from day to day, talking to a mental health professional may be needed (Ariel and Naseef 2003).

THE SIBLINGS

The relationship with our sibling can be the longest lasting family relationship we have and therefore one of the most important. In neurotypical families the course of the sibling relationship changes over time; there are often intense relationships during childhood, more disengaged relationships during the young adult years, and a re-intensification of the sibling bond during midlife and older age (Seltzer *et al.* 2005). The sibling relationship can have a different course for a sibling with a brother or sister with ASD.

Parents are very aware that having a family member with ASD can be challenging and they worry about how the stress of living with ASD will affect the siblings. Parents, and other family members and friends, may be concerned about the lack of attention the siblings may be getting and how the child with ASD's behavior may be affecting the siblings. Parents are sad about the loss of the sibling relationship they imagined and wanted for their children. With all of these concerns, it is very hard for parents to imagine that growing up with a brother or sister with ASD can be a positive experience.

I worried about how this experience might impact the lives of Eric's siblings. But I've learned over the years that if parents are worried, that means they are sensitive to the needs of the siblings and are probably doing all the right things to compensate for the challenges the siblings may be experiencing. Recognizing the potential difficulties siblings might face may be half the battle.

Parents can be the best role model for the siblings. How we accept the difficulties of this experience serves as an example for our other children.

In fact, the key to your family culture is how you treat the child that tests you the most. When you can show unconditional love to your most difficult child, others know that your love for them is also unconditional. (Covey 1997, p.261)

Michael Powers reminds parents in his book, *Children with Autism: A Parent's Guide* (1989), that growing up with a sibling with ASD may not be as unique and terrible as they fear.

> Your child's autism will definitely affect the way she relates to her brothers and sisters and the way they relate to her. Do not assume, however, that all these ways will be bad. Far from it. Having a sibling with autism is stressful and enriching, exasperating and fun, distressing and rewarding. In other words, it is not that different from being the brother or sister of any other child. (Powers 1989, p.123)

Siblings are most likely to adjust well when their parents adjust well, when their parents' marriage is strong and supportive, and when the family is involved with all the children (O'Brien and Daggett 2006). Parents have to realize that siblings experience many of the same feelings about their brother or sister that their parents do. Emotions like love, fear, frustration, pride, guilt, anger, and ambivalence may all be present (Morrell and Palmer 2006).

It is very common for siblings to be disappointed and wish their autistic sibling were "normal." Children with autism typically don't meet the siblings' expectations as playmates. They may be disappointed that their sibling can't or won't play with them. After consistently being rejected, the sibling may give up trying to play with their sibling with ASD.

My daughter was two and a half years younger than her brother Eric. Play was not the immediate issue. Her challenge was just to get Eric to notice and respond to her at all. Eric responded to her as he did to other children. He didn't seem to know she was there and definitely didn't see her as someone to connect with socially. She was incredibly persistent and constantly "in his face" to get him to respond to her. Eventually, it was like a light bulb went off in Eric's head and he suddenly realized that Sarah was somewhat entertaining and he might want to pay attention to her sometimes. That was a defining moment in their relationship and in Eric's ability to recognize the positives of social interactions with others.

Sometimes the sibling may move into more of a caretaker role, rather than a playmate. This is natural as they may see their brother or sister needing help. Older sisters especially tend to gravitate into a caretaker role for their younger sibling with a disability (Harris and Glasberg 2003). This can be problematic, however, if they take too much responsibility for their sibling with ASD.

Being the oldest, I became like a second mommy to Kristy. A big responsibility for anybody, but I loved it… I didn't always grasp it so much then, but as I grew up I realized I gave up a lot to play such a large part in Kristy's upbringing… I did not realize until I got older how lonely I was growing up. (Ariel and Naseef 2006, p.142)

I think the thing that worries me most about Art is how he is going to feel about Jack as they grow up together. Here is Art, a little guy at age five, telling his big brother Jack, who is eleven, how to do things. I mean, what is he going to think about that as he gets older? Big brothers are supposed to take care of little guys, not the other way around. I'm concerned that it must be confusing to Art. (Harris and Glasberg 2003, p.25)

Justin is such a terrific kid. Sometimes I think he is almost too good. He spends so much time with his sister, Allie, who has autism. He acts like it is his job to do everything for her. I don't want him to resent that someday—to feel like she stole his childhood. I appreciate his help, but I don't want him to overdo. I'm not sure how much help is too much. (Harris and Glasberg 2003, p.26)

Children should not be expected to bear major responsibilities for the physical care of their sibling with ASD. It is easy for parents to start relying on a sibling for help, but it is not healthy for the sibling to be responsible for too much. Providing some help is okay. Helping take care of a sibling need not be harmful when it is balanced with opportunities for other activities. Every child should contribute to the welfare of his or her family, but the child should not have a major role as a caretaker.

Siblings may become especially worried about their brother or sister with ASD and become overly protective. Even younger siblings may step into the role of "protector" with their brother or sister. This can be a positive behavior as long as the sibling is not overly consumed with this responsibility. The parents should encourage the sibling to talk about their concerns. They should remind the sibling that the parents will keep the child with ASD safe and it is not the sibling's responsibility alone. As the sibling gets older, he or she may also worry about the autistic sibling's future. There should be open discussions about the future of the child with ASD with the whole family, siblings included.

Children may try to compensate for their autistic sibling's issues by overachieving. They may put unrealistic expectations on themselves to achieve in academics or sports. Some siblings feel that more is expected of them because they do not have a disability. They want to please their parents and may feel the need to excel because their sibling with ASD cannot do as well. To prevent this from happening, parents need to have realistic expectations for their neurotypical children. Parents also may need to remind the siblings that there is no pressure to compensate for their brother or sister's challenges.

It is normal for siblings to resent all the attention their brother or sister may need. The family may be overwhelmed with taking care of the needs of the child with autism and siblings can feel excluded or jealous about the attention their brother or sister is getting. Parents may need to remind the sibling that just because they have to give their brother or sister more time, it doesn't mean they are giving them more love. Siblings just want to feel "special" too.

I like what Heather Featherstone says:

> Listening to normal brothers and sisters talk about family life, I am struck by a paradox about disability. In the world outside the family, in school and in the neighborhood, children long to fit in, to resemble everyone else. In these contexts…a sibling's disability stigmatizes them as different. Inside the family, however, each child wants to be special. (Featherstone 1980, p.47)

Sometimes my daughter would see me "working" with Eric (which looked a lot like playing) and get jealous. This was understandable because we were often doing fun things like puzzles and reading books. Of course she felt left out! I realized I needed to make time to "work" with Sarah too and make her feel special. So I would set aside some time and some baskets of activities that were just for Sarah. Later, we introduced her into doing "work" activities with Eric. It was great because Eric liked doing these structured activities and was willing to have Sarah participate. And Sarah learned more about how to play with Eric.

Children, just like parents, often do not understand their autistic sibling's behaviors. They may not understand why their brother or sister is disciplined differently or allowed certain behaviors that they aren't. They may get angry when their sibling breaks one of their toys or disrupts a family activity. Parents need to explain as much as they can to the sibling about why these behaviors happen. It is also important for the sibling to have an "autism-free zone" if possible in the home; a place where their things are safe and they can be alone when they want (Sicile-Kira 2004).

One way parents can help with some of the resentment the siblings may be feeling is by encouraging the siblings to have interests outside of the family and arranging special times to pursue those interests. The parents may have to "divide and conquer," but that's okay. It is not always necessary to do everything as a family. Sometimes it makes more sense to have one parent stay home with the child with ASD and the other parent take the sibling out for their own special time.

Over the years we were raising our children, Sarah had dance classes and performances and Philip, fours years younger than Sarah, had karate and Boy Scouts. These were activities that were their own, that they didn't have to share with their brother with autism. My husband and I set aside these times to spend alone with them without their brother. The whole family, extended family included, was able to celebrate their accomplishments in these activities. I think that helped them to understand that sometimes Eric took a lot of our attention, but they were equally as important in the family. If it is difficult to find the time to do this, remember that it may not be the amount of time that is spent with the sibling but the quality of that time that is important.

Parents may have to be creative in order to find the time to spend with the neurotypical sibling. They can combine doing errands with doing something special with the sibling. Or while the child with ASD is having therapy, parents can do something alone with the sibling. If possible, arrange an occasional overnight, just the parent and the sibling. If the family is going on a vacation, consider bringing along a caregiver to help with the child with ASD to free up more time to spend with the siblings. If time is chosen wisely, there are ways to show special attention to the sibling who may be feeling neglected.

> To make time for the other children, I either take them out for something fun one at a time, or get my husband to take our child with special needs out, so we can have fun at home...
> I also try to make sure that I compliment the other children as they try to help with our special needs child or help me. (Baskin and Fawcett 2006, p.264)

Siblings also may feel guilty about a number of things. They may feel guilty that their brother or sister was affected but they were spared. They may feel guilty because they can enjoy certain things their sibling with ASD cannot. They may love their brother or sister but resent the extra attention they get and feel guilty about that resentment. They may get angry toward their sibling and later feel guilty for that anger.

> I did not know anyone else with a family member who was "special." I remember thinking how horrible I was for feeling jealousy for things that my sister *needed* and I only *wanted*. I was afraid to talk about it with my parents, afraid they would think I was a rotten sister for feeling all these feelings—some good...and some not so good. (Ariel and Naseef 2006, p.143)

Siblings may also be embarrassed by their sibling with ASD. This is a normal response for siblings, and for parents, especially when the child has unusual behaviors that attract attention. The odd behaviors of the child with ASD in public can be difficult for the sibling to handle, especially if there are friends or peers nearby. It is difficult for the sibling to handle the questions, stares or comments from their friends. Siblings may want to have friends over to their house but may be embarrassed by the behaviors of their brother or sister.

> Then there were times when my friends would ask if we could come to my house and I'd have to come up with excuses why not. "My mom is sick." "We have company." "We are remodeling our house so there isn't room." Anything I could think of so that my friends wouldn't have to see my brother. I wouldn't have to explain him. (Ariel and Naseef 2006, p.147)

If possible, parents should try to arrange time for friends to come over when the child with ASD will not be able to disrupt the sibling's time with their friends. You want your home to be welcoming to others and the sibling to feel less isolated.

Siblings often find themselves having to educate others about ASD. Depending on the age of the sibling and how shy or outgoing they may be, this can be very difficult. Parents can educate the sibling and help them come up with set responses they can give when questions arise. Not only does educating them help with responding to the comments of others, but also it helps the sibling understand their brother or sister with ASD. "Combating ignorance and educating others is an important skill for a sibling. However, it is more important that he understand autism for his own emotional well-being" (Harris and Glasberg 2003, p.56).

If the sibling does not get enough information to help them understand ASD, they may have fears or fantasies that are not realistic. They may blame themselves for their sibling's condition. They may worry that their autistic sibling will die or that they themselves can "catch" the autism. Siblings do not typically have the opportunities that parents have to get information. That is why it is so important for parents to have good communication with the sibling about ASD and how it affects their brother or sister.

> They both understand that I have to do things differently with the other sibling. I am completely open and honest with my children. It helps if they know what to expect, when and why to expect it. (Baskin and Fawcett 2006, p.258)

Parents may feel the need to protect the sibling by not sharing information that may be difficult to hear. But children need information to be able to adapt. They already know that their sibling is different. They need to know what it is and how the family is going to help the sibling with ASD. If parents try to keep the diagnosis a secret, the siblings could be made to believe that ASD is something to be ashamed of.

When sharing information with siblings it is important to remember that children process things differently at different ages. What the parents are sharing and what the children are grasping may be totally different (Harris and Glasberg 2003). A simple way of discussing the ASD with the siblings is to emphasize the positive traits and strengths of the sibling with ASD. When explaining my son's diagnosis of autism to his brother and sister, I focused on the things he could do that other kids his age couldn't do. I also discussed the things each of the siblings could do that Eric couldn't do, pointing out that we all have strengths and weaknesses. Eric's autism was just one of the things that made him unique.

It is easy to want to wait until the siblings show interest in learning more before starting this dialogue. But parents should take the lead rather than wait for questions (O'Brien and Daggett 2006). The conversation needs to be ongoing and frequent and consistent with the age and the level of understanding of the sibling. It reminds me of the "sex talk" when the parent gives the child information they can handle for their age, knowing that they will need more conversations over time to give more information.

Parents need to create an open door policy for discussions about ASD, starting as young as possible. "Make autism as acceptable to discuss as what will be served for dinner" (Harris and Glasberg 2003, p.48). And parents need to be open to *all* comments, not just the positive ones.

> I gave Michael and Patrick encouragement to honestly express their feelings, so long as they were positive. I wasn't so good with the negatives. I am sure throughout much of their childhood they sensed my ambivalence about hearing those negatives and modified their responses to my questions accordingly... It was hard to hear about the difficulty of living with Justin because I was afraid their emotions were the tip of the iceberg and the negative feelings were much deeper than the positive. I was afraid it meant they did not love him. (Morrell and Palmer 2006, pp.38–39)

Parents should be open about their own feelings and allow the siblings to complain if they need to. Parents will need to be prepared for intense emotions coming out. It may take some effort to focus on being a good listener and being non-judgmental. The sibling needs to feel comfortable sharing their true feelings. The parents want them to know they can come to them anytime about how they are feeling. Parents are confused when they are first learning about ASD, so it is important to let the sibling know that it is normal to feel confused.

It is also normal to feel sad, angry, etc. and the parent has to allow the siblings to express those emotions. There are quite a few books written about ASD that are targeted to children and some that are written specifically about the sibling experience. These books may help the sibling feel less alone in this experience.

Another important way to support the siblings is to acknowledge the contributions that they make every day living with a brother or sister with ASD. Parents, and family members and friends, can acknowledge the difficulties and sacrifices the sibling may be making. Let them know you recognize that it is difficult at times and you appreciate all they do in the family.

It is also important to strengthen the siblings' support system. Support can come from other family members or friends or support programs specifically related to the disability. Finding a support group for families of children with ASD may open up opportunities for the siblings to meet other siblings and be with other families. It allows them to see that there are other families going through similar experiences.

There may also be support groups specifically for siblings in your community. Meeting other siblings of children with ASD can help the sibling feel less isolated. "Sibshops" is a program developed in the United States by the Sibling Support Project and is a national model that offers siblings of children with special needs peer support and education (www.siblingsupport.org). During these workshops, information and discussion activities are combined with recreational activities (Meyer 1995). Parents may want to look for these kinds of sibling support opportunities in their community. If siblings are really struggling, and the parents have tried many of the strategies I've suggested, it may be necessary to reach out for professional counseling.

We've talked about all the difficulties surrounding siblings living with a brother or sister with ASD. But there are many positives of this experience.

My sister gives me unconditional love all the time. She cheers me up when I'm sad. I love teaching her new things. She helps me see the world in different ways. (Baskin and Fawcett 2006, p.255)

A sibling can be the best teacher for your child with ASD. I found that Eric's brother and sister were great role models for him over the years, especially during their teen years. They exposed him to the music and clothes that teenagers like and they became a social network of sorts for him.

What may be a very difficult relationship between siblings and the child with ASD when they are young may turn out to be a very positive relationship when they are adults. Maturity and experience can change the perspective of the sibling toward the brother or sister with ASD. When Eric was young he pretty much ignored his brother and sister. As they all got older, friendships developed. Now that they are all adults they like each other's company and they do things together and have a good relationship.

It is helpful for parents to remind themselves that not everything the sibling does is in response to having a brother or sister with ASD. Jealousy, sibling rivalry, competition, etc. are universal. Every family with more than one child deals with sibling issues at times and struggles to balance their attentions to all the children. And all families have difficulties they must live with. It may be taking care of an aging parent, losing a job, divorce, an illness in the family, etc. Siblings know other families going through difficulties and their personal life with a sibling with ASD may not seem that different from their friends' lives.

Both of Eric's siblings have told me that they never felt their life was especially difficult or different. In fact they are quick to remind me of their friends who grew up in families with more problems than ours. It was helpful for me to realize that indeed all families have their struggles at times and autism doesn't necessarily predetermine a sad or isolating family life. (Morrell and Palmer 2006, p.52)

While research is mixed, most studies show siblings of children with disabilities are indistinguishable from their peers. They report few differences in behavior, self-esteem, or competence. Researchers note positive effects too—such as maturity, responsibility, and cooperation. Other studies find siblings of children with disabilities and chronic illnesses show more warmth, tolerance of the differences of others, empathy, affection and helpfulness as compared to siblings of non-disabled children. (Baskin and Fawcett 2006, p.263)

Having…as a brother has helped me to develop a strength of character that I believe would be lacking if he had not come into my life…taught me to never underestimate the power of optimism and hope [and] that labels are quite meaningless when it comes to predicting the ability of people to create magical and powerful lives. (Donnelly et al. 2000, p.199)

In Thomas Powell and Peggy Ogle's book, *Brothers and Sisters: A Special Part of Exceptional Families* (1985), they describe comments made by a panel of adult siblings of individuals with a variety of disabilities. The adult siblings describe the benefits they have received from the experience of living with a brother or sister with a disability. They said they were more understanding of human problems; they accept people better and are less judgmental and more easygoing. They also reported that through this experience they learned to teach and they developed more patience. The siblings all commented that their family members have become closer and more open and honest with each other (Powell and Ogle 1985). The panel also gave a number of strategies for parents. Here are some of the suggestions they gave:

Be open and honest.
Value each child individually.
Be fair in terms of discipline, attention and resources.
Accept the disability.
Let siblings settle their own differences.
Welcome other children and friends into the home.
Praise siblings.
Recognize you are the most important teacher of your children.
Recognize the uniqueness of your family and feel good about your family.
Involve the siblings.
Require the child with disabilities to do as much for himself as possible.
Recognize each child's unique qualities and contribution.
Recognize special stress times for siblings and plan to minimize negative effects.
Teach the sibling to interact with the child with disabilities.
Provide opportunities for normal family life and activities.
Don't expect the sibling to be a saint.

(Powell and Ogle 1985, pp.177–182)

Lastly, it is important to remember that the lifelong relationship between siblings includes the future, when parents are no longer around. Siblings worry about what their role will be with their brother or sister with ASD in the future. For that reason it is important that parents have an open dialogue with the siblings about the future of the family member with ASD. Parents may instinctively want to protect the siblings from this kind of conversation but it is better to involve them in the process. Many adult siblings have told me that they wished they had been included in more of the decision making about their sibling's residential and work options. Adult siblings often feel unprepared for the responsibilities they eventually have in taking care of their brother or sister with ASD. The best thing parents can do is to respect the siblings' perspectives and opinions, involve them in their adult sibling's life, and help them understand what their responsibilities may be in the future for their brother or sister with ASD.

Chapter 4

EXTENDED FAMILY
AND FRIENDS

There are an estimated 1 million to 1.5 million individuals living with ASD in the United States (Autism Society of America 2009). In 2007 in the United Kingdom there were estimated to be 650,000 individuals with autism. Bob Wright, co-founder of Autism Speaks, reported that approximately 67 million people are affected by autism around the world (Early Signs of Autism 2010).

Autism affects not only 67 million people, but also all the family members and friends of those individuals. From the 1.5 million individuals with ASD in the United States, we can assume that there are somewhere between 3 million and 6 million immediate family members and many more extended family members and friends who care about them. Friends and family can play a crucial role in providing the support that families of children with ASD need. However, family relationships and family history are often complicated and autism can be challenging to understand. These factors often make it difficult for healthy supportive relationships to exist beyond the immediate family.

A study done by the Interactive Autism Network (IAN) Project through Autism Speaks found 43 percent of fathers and nearly 50 percent of mothers reported a negative impact on extended family relationships from having a child with ASD. For many families in the study the impact was mixed, with some relatives in denial and dismissive of the diagnosis, while others were helpful and supportive (Autism Speaks 2009).

Most people have a history of both good and bad experiences with their family members. Relationships with family members are often complicated and can be complicated even more when autism enters the picture. If the parents are close to an extended family member, chances are that relationship will continue to thrive even after the autism. However, if the quality of the relationship has always been tenuous, autism can make it more so. There may be disagreements about the actual diagnosis. There may be disagreements about the parenting style or what kinds of interventions are chosen for the child. If the child has challenging behaviors, visits to family or involvement in family functions may be limited. Extended family members who don't see the child frequently or don't understand the day-to-day difficulties of taking care of a child with ASD may not understand the decisions the parents are making (Morrell and Palmer 2006).

OBSTACLES TO SUPPORT FROM FAMILY AND FRIENDS

One of the major obstacles to receiving support from family and friends is the parents' avoidance of the discussion of the diagnosis and the child's needs. Family members and friends may be frustrated because the parents aren't sharing information or telling others about the challenges they are living with. Having little information makes it difficult for family and friends to know how to help.

There are many reasons why a parent may not feel comfortable opening up to others. Disclosing about the diagnosis makes the parent have to admit to themselves, and to others, that this is really happening. Telling people makes parents have to face the difficult reality of their situation. Parents also may not want to disclose because they fear being misunderstood, judged or pitied. Parents may feel that telling others is an invasion of their privacy or the child's privacy. Some parents may feel too emotional to say the words out loud. They may not be talking about it with others because they don't want to lose control of the emotions they are holding inside.

I isolated myself that first week and stayed at home and cried and avoided the people who meant the most to me. They wanted to help me but if I saw them or spoke to them it was too hard to keep up the protective wall I had built around myself. (Morrell and Palmer 2006, pp.16–17)

I called some people that are close to us and explained what was going on… That was a really tough time, but we got through it, and our family is slowly coming out of denial. It sucks to tell people, but I think that it is better to enlighten them in the end, and you may be surprised who comes out of the woodwork to support you. I just think that in order for me to fully accept my son (work in progress) I needed to let go of the burden of holding it all on my own. (BabyCenter 2011)

Parents may not want to tell others for fear of causing them pain and sadness.

I hated being the messenger of bad news. Adding worry and sadness to their lives increased the weight of the sadness I carried in my own. When I assumed the messenger role, it drained too much emotional energy from me. I needed all of my emotional reserves to take care of the family at hand. (Morrell and Palmer 2006, p.67)

I remember I gave them little information because they were not in a "place" to help me and I knew they would worry, and call to talk about it and create more stress than support. (Parent of J)

And sometimes explaining it to others is difficult because the parent doesn't know *how* to explain it. They may still be trying to understand it themselves and may not feel knowledgeable enough to explain it to others. They may not feel comfortable answering the questions people may have.

> Explaining all this to his inner circle—when we had so much information to absorb ourselves—was difficult. While family members have been supportive, Will's behavior is even baffling to those closest to him. (Ariel and Naseef 2006, p.41)

> I tried to explain the diagnosis which was pretty murky and kept changing. It was hard for me to understand what to do, so I know it must have been hard for someone else to understand. (Parent of D)

> I spoke about the diagnosis in simple terminology—as I also didn't have a lot of knowledge. I did not give examples of other children nor was I able to offer prognosis. I gave info in "chunks" as I learned more. (Parent of B)

> If I try to talk to someone who I have to educate before I vent, I'm too exhausted to vent by the time I'm done educating them! (Autism Speaks 2009, p.3)

Because disclosing about the diagnosis can be so difficult for parents, they often carefully choose who they tell and who they don't. Some of the questions parents may ask themselves include, does this person need to know? How close are they to my child and to me? How will they react? And will they treat this information with sensitivity and respect (Stillman 2010)?

> My mom and sisters are the only people in my family that know. I don't know how to tell my dad or my brother, or anyone for that matter. I already know what my dad will say, so I honestly

don't see myself telling him anything in the near future. We rarely see him anyway. (BabyCenter 2011)

I told my sisters more than my brother. I did not think he would understand or that he might challenge the diagnosis and blame me for it. (Parent of C)

Some friends were more open to trying to understand. Others were busy raising their own families and really couldn't relate to what we were facing. Information was given on a need-to-know basis generally, and only when we were asked or to prepare folks for what might happen when we were together. (Parent of J)

One hurtful thing I remember during the time of the initial diagnosis is learning that our "news" had been shared at a party with friends. The only thing I felt was extremely important to me was my privacy and my "choice" about who I told and when I told. Learning that this had been shared like cocktail party conversation did not make me feel good and was hurtful to both my husband and myself. I didn't like the idea of people outside of my family (and especially ones who had no idea what I was going through) to be feeling sorry for me. (Parent of W)

Not all extended family members or friends need to know about the ASD. If they don't have much contact with the child or the family or the parents don't think they will understand, maybe it's better not to tell them at all. Disclosing is often based on the "need to know" as described in this parent's comments:

I only explain it when people notice that he is different, or I guess just not responding how typical children do. So when we visit extended family that we never really see, and they keep commenting to me about this or that thing he is doing or not doing, that's when I say, "He was recently diagnosed with autism, so one of the things he struggles with is xyz." (BabyCenter 2011)

Some parents seem to have no problem telling people about the diagnosis and easily recognize the need to reach out for support from family and friends.

We just got diagnosed and all of our family and friends know. I spent the 2 days after the diagnosis informing people. We need the extra support from our family and friends. And they have been awesome!!!! (BabyCenter 2011)

I told my family immediately—both sides—as this was my first child and I had no idea what was going on and needed guidance. I openly talk about it—and, in so doing, one of my best friends from high school reached out to me as her son was diagnosed last week. (BabyCenter 2011)

Before making decisions about disclosing it is important to consider the child's feelings. If the child with ASD can understand the concept of sharing the diagnosis with others and what that may mean, they should be a part of the decision. Does the child want others to know? Can the child "pass" when in settings with other children without ASD? Will it help the child for others to know about the diagnosis?

Another obstacle to receiving support from family members and friends is the reluctance parents may have to ask for help or accept help from others. Accepting help from family members can be complicated. Part of the developmental growth of a young family is to establish their independence by separating from their families. Just when the parents have started that separation, a child with autism may require a step back to their family for support.

Women, especially, are used to being the helpers, not the "helpees." Asking for help can make them feel vulnerable and needy. How to negotiate accepting help and maintaining independence is a tricky balance.

One of the hardest things for me was letting my family know that I needed help from them. My mom said I always seemed to have everything under control and she didn't want to intrude. Once I told her I could use the help, she was great. (Harris and Glasberg 2003, p.123)

I do not accept help well. I am uncomfortable letting others see what feels like my failings or weaknesses. I don't like admitting I even need help, much less accepting that help when it is offered. I know it is healthy and normal to reach out to someone for help when things are difficult, but it totally goes against my nature to do so. As much as I hated it, when Eric was first diagnosed and Sarah was a baby, I realized I couldn't do it all. I had to accept the help that was being offered. Fortunately, my family and my husband's family were offering to help. I'm not sure I would have been able to initiate asking them. Over time I realized that needing their help didn't mean I had failed in any way. I was human and could only do so much. (Morrell and Palmer 2006, p.120)

A parent may need permission to ask for help.

She looked me in the eye and told me that while all my siblings have children, none has had to deal with the kind of stress I have... She told me they were all so proud of me, and that it was okay if I reached out and asked for help sometimes. Realizing that my brother and sisters thought of me as someone they could respect, gave me the strength to move forward and acknowledge that I was dealing with exceptional circumstances. (Brodey 2007, p.53)

REACTIONS TO THE DIAGNOSIS

Just like the parents of the child with ASD, family members and friends are going to process the diagnosis in different ways and at different rates. Relatives and friends may go through their own journey—from not accepting the diagnosis, recognizing the truth, learning how to interact with the child and the family, and becoming an advocate for the child with ASD. They too may experience a significant amount of stress and grief from this experience. Their reactions to the diagnosis are going to be influenced by many factors including their knowledge and acceptance of disabilities, their culture, their faith, the amount of support they have, and their relationship with the parents of the child with ASD.

> [The reactions] varied a lot… Some were disbelieving because he "looked so normal," was "so smart," was such a "beautiful child…" Others were sad and sympathetic. (Parent of P)

There are many family members and friends who, upon hearing about the diagnosis, are immediately going to offer the words of encouragement and support that the parents need. There are also family members and friends who will not know immediately what to do and what to say and may react in ways that are not helpful. Mistakes can be made. Initial reactions may be based on misinformation about ASD or in response to the emotions the family member or friend may be feeling. It is important to discuss the reactions that are not very helpful so friends and relatives can know what not to do as well as what to do if someone they love needs their support.

The initial reaction I hear about the most from parents is the family member or friend who disagrees with or trivializes the diagnosis. They may make comments like, "I'm sure he will be fine" or "I'm sure that's not what it is."

> They say, "He's fine! All kids develop differently. Your Dad didn't talk till he was 3." My dad also didn't spin toy car wheels

for hours on end, bang his head on the wall and gag himself for fun. (Autism Speaks 2009, p.3)

The most common reactions were that she could not have it [autism]. That was hard to handle. I know they meant well, but it did not help. (Parent of C)

My father was not willing to accept it and thought my son was just spoiled—it created a lot of tension when we visited. My father mostly saw a rambunctious child whom we couldn't control and assumed he just needed some discipline. For example, he refused to "child-proof" the kitchen and felt we just had to teach him not to open cabinets, etc. (Needless to say, this was not very successful and put us all constantly on edge.) (Parent of P)

Our family was shocked, sad, and sympathetic, though my family had a harder time accepting it and seemed to feel that he would "grow out of it" and kept pointing to all the things he had done in the past (but was no longer doing) and kept saying how smart he seemed. We always felt supported but felt that they didn't really understand. (Parent of J)

With this kind of reaction, the person is trying to convince the parents that the diagnosis can't possibly be true. Because they care about the parents, they don't want to see them in pain. They may see it as their duty to make the parents feel better by convincing them that they must be wrong, the professionals must be wrong, there must be another explanation. The family member or friend actually doesn't know what to say. They are scared too, and they just want to make their loved one feel better. In reality, disagreeing with the news is not helpful for parents. Parents are struggling with accepting the diagnosis too and what they really need is someone to help them understand rather than encourage more doubts.

We told people about DS's diagnosis when he received one. I'm glad that we did, but it wasn't easy. Most people just don't seem to know what to do. We received a lot of "Oh, he's fine" comments. I think people want to reassure, but that's actually pretty frustrating when you're really worried. (BabyCenter 2011)

The friend or family member may deny that anything is wrong to avoid facing their own sorrow. As stated earlier, parents may be in denial about the diagnosis when they are not ready emotionally to accept it. This can happen to anyone who loves the child and is not ready to face the reality of the situation. Family members or friends may not be able to face the grief they are feeling, and denying the diagnosis protects them from confronting their feelings.

Disagreement with the diagnosis may be a reaction based on a lack of knowledge about ASD. Most family members and friends are going to have a limited knowledge of the spectrum of autism. The picture of autism in their mind may be the non-verbal child sitting in the corner rocking, or Raymond, the character in the movie *Rain Man* who showed incredible savant skills. If the child with ASD doesn't look like either of those pictures, the family member may have trouble recognizing the child's disability. If the disability is physically invisible, as it typically is with ASD, they may not see anything different or wrong with the child initially. The more subtle expression of ASD in children with Asperger syndrome or high functioning autism may make it even more difficult for family members to recognize and accept. If they don't spend much time around the child they may not see the behaviors the parents see.

Some family members or friends may feel so strongly that it can't be ASD that they don't believe the parents should be looking into a diagnosis at all. When parents start having questions and concerns about their child and family members or friends are disagreeing with their search for answers, it only makes it harder for the parents. The truth is, it is actually very brave for parents to ask the tough questions when they don't really want to know the answers.

My family does not believe in ASD, so they do not agree with finding her services, and feel that her "out of control" behavior simply shows my lack as a parent. (Autism Speaks 2009, p.4)

Some of the child's odd behaviors or delays can be misunderstood as "typical" behaviors, especially if the person does not understand ASD. Many children have a delay in speaking but don't end up with ASD. Many children like playing alone at times or are shy. Kids often like to line up toys or want to play with the same toy all the time. Many children get obsessed with certain videos and want to watch them over and over. It is understandable that sometimes extended family and friends can find reasons why everything the child does could fall in the "normal" range. However, the difference for the child with ASD is that these behaviors or delays interfere in a major way with the child's ability to function in their environment. Parents usually see more of the big picture and have a better understanding of how their child is different from neurotypical children the same age.

My mom has been great but she is in denial. She keeps telling me that there is nothing wrong with her and that she is perfect. This makes me feel bad because I also think she's perfect. I don't think that anyone is saying Marley is imperfect, but she definitely is behind other kids her age and lacks a lot of social skills. (BabyCenter 2011)

Helping family members and friends understand ASD can help them be more accepting of the diagnosis.

We were very fortunate that Eric's grandparents lived nearby. I found that it meant a great deal to them to be included in my learning process as I was trying to understand autism and how to help Eric. I would share many of the reports and evaluations on Eric with his grandparents. I gave them articles I read about autism that I thought would be meaningful to them. I would take them with me to occasional support groups and conferences. They watched me work with him at home and were able to observe him sometimes at occupational and speech therapy sessions. I think it helped them understand Eric and it made them more accepting and supportive of us in our parenting decisions. They also felt more involved and more capable of helping us and Eric. (Morrell and Palmer 2006, p.67)

Educating family members and friends about ASD and how it affects the child is important. However, parents need to be careful when deciding what to share with relatives and friends. The clinical descriptions within diagnostic reports can be emotionally difficult to read. Parts of the reports might be helpful but some parts may not. Parents also need to be selective of the books or articles they recommend. Some books about autism are overly technical or depressing. Before sharing something to read with the family member or friend, parents need to think about that person's possible emotional response and their level of interest and knowledge.

Some people may have difficulty facing the diagnosis because of their past history with disabilities. Older family members or friends may have a very different way of looking at disabilities in general, based on the way they were raised and the way society treated disabilities many years ago. In the past, if someone looked "normal" than they were expected to succeed in school; if they didn't, they were considered lazy (Zachry 2008). People didn't understand learning disabilities or "invisible" disabilities and if a child acted out it was assumed that they were not disciplined well.

Not that many years ago children with disabilities were isolated from other children in school. Children didn't grow up attending class and socializing with people who had differences, unlike today where children with physical and developmental disabilities are in classes with other children. Disabilities were much more stigmatized in the past and families often didn't talk about the family member with a disability. For a grandparent who grew up during that time, they may fear how others will react and the kind of life the child may have because of their disability.

> She didn't discuss the diagnosis with her friends. Mother functions in the "if you can't say anything nice, then don't say anything" world and only shares good news with friends. So, I got the feeling she was embarrassed. (Parent of D speaking about her mother)

Another reaction to the diagnosis can be to avoid contact with the child or the family.

> Sometimes, out of fear, family and friends pull away from us after our child is diagnosed, convincing themselves that they're being protective, by shielding the child from their ignorance of ASDs—when in reality, they're hurting the ones they love. Some pull away because they feel rejected; the child doesn't respond when they call her name or doesn't let them hug her. (Exkorn 2005, p.263)

> One of the toughest things for me about my son's autism has been how my family has reacted. When my parents heard that Dick had autism they just seemed to disappear. They never offer to sit with him. My sister-in-law asked me to leave Dick at home when they had a family party and invited all the other children. Those things just go right to my heart. So, I don't see much of my family, but it hurts a lot. (Harris and Glasberg 2003, p.124)

Invitations to social gatherings may stop. Friends or family members without children, or those who have children without special needs, may feel uncomfortable around a person with ASD. They may have trouble knowing how to respond around children with language delays or social and behavioral difficulties. Some parents may not want their neurotypical children playing with a child with ASD, as if the disorder might be contagious.

> My son has also been snubbed by other members of our family, who have kids the same age as he is. He doesn't get invited over to play at their houses, or to their birthday parties. (Myers *et al.* 2009, p.680)

This kind of reaction is very hurtful for the parents and the child with ASD. However, there are ways that parents can respond that can help in these situations. The family member or friend who is excluding the child or distancing themselves from the family may just need more information. They may assume since the child has social difficulties, they wouldn't enjoy a social activity or that the parents would not want them to participate. Parents can try to clear up this misperception that is often made. Family members or friends may need to understand why the child ignores them or doesn't respond; that it is because of the ASD and not a personal rejection. They may need to learn strategies to improve their interactions with the child, such as what to say and do to engage the child.

Many of the stories I hear of negative reactions from family members and friends revolve around assigning blame for the disorder and making judgments about the way the parents are parenting their child with ASD. The following comment is from a grandmother who has regrets about her reactions:

> Such a trauma for all of us... Never in my life did I believe I'd have to go through something like this...I am disappointed with myself...I feel I should have been able to do more, to be more understanding... Sometimes I would be judgmental or critical, and they would feel I did not trust them and realize that they were doing their best... I never realized how much it hurt them... I have had to learn a lot, a major life experience, but we have all learnt to deal with it and with each other. (Katz and Kessel 2002, p.124)

Family members may blame one of the parents for the role their genes may have played in determining the child's diagnosis. They may blame the child's autism on the way the parents are raising the child; they spoil the child, they don't discipline them enough, etc. Offering constant advice to the parents about parenting their child is usually an indication that the family member or friend blames the child's disability on poor parenting skills.

My family turned against me, and has made it clear that they believe that I caused my son's autism. (Myers *et al.* 2009, p.680)

An Easter holiday right after Rick was officially diagnosed stands out in my mind. It was the first time we had been together with my husband's "large family." The topic turned to Rick and "his problem." The general consensus was that it must have been something we (my husband and I) did—not things like hurting him, but things like not lying him down on the floor on a blanket and allowing him to develop. I left in tears not to return to a family gathering for months. We never had an apology from anyone either. (Brower and Wright 1986, p.8)

There was considerable strife with relatives who expressed the view that our son was merely spoiled and that we were inadequate parents. (Myers *et al.* 2009, p.680)

One of my nieces once told me that her father (my brother-in-law) told the family that if he could have my son for six months— he'd be talking. This was extremely painful to hear, especially coming from the mouth of a young child. (Parent of B)

My mother feels that we as parents have failed to discipline our children. She attributes all of my autistic daughter's bad behavior to our failure as parents, and none of it to autism. (Autism Speaks 2009, p.3)

These statements are difficult to read and it is hard to understand how people can be so insensitive. I can't excuse all the hurtful comments and actions of others. But I try to remind myself and encourage parents to remember that most extended family members and friends don't know exactly what to say and how to react. They too are trying to adjust to the information and (let's hope) want to do all the right things to support the parents. Mistakes can be made, comments may not always be helpful, but many people who care about the child and the family have their hearts in the right place.

> People either ignore it, downplay it ("Oh, I'm sure everything will be fine") or are very sympathetic ("Oh, I am *so* sorry!"). None of these responses is particularly comforting or helpful. However, I try to empathize with the other person. Before my son was diagnosed, would I have known what to say to someone in my position? Probably not. (BabyCenter 2011)

> I wish they had reached out more, but I realize they just didn't know what to do or say…heck, I didn't know what to do or say! (Parent of J)

In some situations, despite all the efforts to build a supportive relationship between family members and friends and the parents and child with ASD, the relationship never improves. For whatever reasons, some people will never understand. Some will never completely accept the child with ASD. Some relationships are not strong enough to survive this experience.

> It was sad that Rob's parents never came to know Justin very well. They never really got over seeing him as "poor Justin," and never saw our life without tragic overtones. In the end, their view of our lives did not cause me much pain. Because I did not rely on them as my main source of emotional support, I did not expect more than they were able to give. (Morrell and Palmer 2006, pp.65–66)

Sometimes parents have to stop worrying about how to change a family member or friend's viewpoint and recognize when there is nothing else they can do. They want their family and friends to support them and to love their child for who he or she is. Parents don't need the added stress of dealing with a family member's or friend's ignorance or stubbornness when they have tried everything they can to involve them and educate them about their child. This mother of three children with disabilities says it well.

> I cannot control my family's acceptance. I can only control my own. (Baskin and Fawcett 2006, p.272)

Some relationships are just too fragile to withstand the challenges that autism brings, and despite the parents' best efforts, the relationship may not survive. It's sad, but it's necessary in some situations for parents to make the decision that allowing a particular family member or friend to be involved is not healthy for the child or for the family. The parents' energies may be more productive when directed towards building on those relationships that are supportive and add to their lives (Morrell and Palmer 2006).

It's helpful to remind ourselves that over time relationships can change. The door to communication should remain open so that contact can be re-established when the time is right. Maybe at some point down the road the relationship can be repaired. When the hectic child-rearing days are over, parents may have more time and energy to put into building relationships. As people mature, as more information is known about ASD, more opportunities may come for better relationships to develop.

> Twenty years later, they're opening up to me. It's been a great bonding experience, and I feel honored that they're sharing. (Aunt of R)

I have been surprised and delighted that as our families have grown up there are more opportunities for extended family members to be involved in Justin's life. As his cousins have become adults, they are able to come to visit. They follow the explosion of autism information in the media and frequently email me articles that provide the latest autism information. They are curious about Justin's life and ask questions about his past and his present. They donate to the causes that improve his life and the lives of other individuals with autism. As Rob and I age, I am encouraged by the chance to expand the circle of family members who care about Justin and may be able to offer him support in the future. (Morrell and Palmer 2006, p.69)

I don't want to imply that all family members and friends react in ways that cause added stress to the parents. There are many family members and friends that react in very positive ways to the news of the diagnosis and are invaluable supports to the family at a very difficult time.

It has brought our family closer as we all try to work with ways to help him. (Myers *et al.* 2009, p.680)

I think we became even closer... She was constantly praising us for the good job we were doing handling his behaviors and seeking professional help and therapy. Her support meant a lot to both of us. (Parent of J speaking about her mother-in-law)

I remember telling a friend whom we hadn't seen in over a year. We calmly rattled off all the details, almost by rote at that point, and she began to cry. She said "How awful for the two of you!" Of course, I then cried too, and I loved her so much for being able to see past the calm exterior and barrage of diagnostic terms, and understand what it had to mean for us. (Parent of P)

I think I am closer to the rest of my family (mom, dad, sisters) because of J, it has pulled us together as a family to create a unit that my son can count on. (Myers *et al.* 2009, p.680)

GRANDPARENTS

Grandparents deserve special attention because of the important role they can play in supporting the family living with ASD. In a survey done by the Interactive Autism Network, it was found that grandparents are often the first to suspect that a child may have autism. They often play a major role in caring for children with ASD once they are diagnosed. Over 36 percent of grandparents reported that they take care of their grandchild at least once a week, and about one in five indicated that they provide regular transportation for the child. In many cases grandparents are adjusting their lifestyle to accommodate their grandchild by moving to be closer to the family or actually living with the grandchild. Nearly all the grandparents involved in the survey said they read or do research to learn more about autism and they participate in fundraising or advocate on behalf of their grandchild with ASD. And most importantly, almost 90 percent said they are closer to their adult child because their grandchild has autism (Diamont 2010).

My son's grandparents played a very important role in his early life and in my survival of those early years following the diagnosis. They helped by babysitting my daughter while I took Eric to his therapy appointments. They would watch our children so my husband and I could go out for "date nights." My mother would often go with me and my children on outings so I would have an extra pair of hands if needed. She also went with us on vacation each year. I realize how fortunate I was to have Eric's grandparents nearby and involved in our family's life. All the grandparents are gone now but my mother was alive to see Eric graduate from college. She was so proud of him and how far he had come and was able to see how the support she gave us over the years made a difference in Eric's life.

The importance of grandparents in our society is becoming increasingly apparent. The number of grandparents is rising due to multiple marriages, people becoming grandparents at a much younger age, and lengthening lifespans. There is a longer time when grandparents and grandchildren may interact. With healthier grandparents there's a greater potential for them to be more active in the lives of their grandchildren (Scherman and Gardner 1995). Over the years I have seen an increase in grandparents attending autism-related support groups and conferences. Many of these grandparents that I've met are actually raising their grandchildren with ASD and are looking for support for themselves and their grandchild.

Grandparents can have a special role in supporting the child with ASD and the family. They are probably more connected to the family than any other extended family member. Their relationship with the parents is one of the most important relationships the parents have. Grandparents who successfully maintain their contact with their grandchildren are typically those who have friendly relations with the grandchild's parents (Scherman and Gardner 1995). However, if the relationship between the parents and grandparents is strained or if the grandparents react in a negative way to the news of the diagnosis, it can create additional burdens on the parents who are trying to cope.

Disclosing the news about the child's diagnosis to the grandparents can be a major concern for the parents. The parents may have mixed emotions, wanting their parents' support and yet worrying about how they will react to the news.

On the day I went to their house with the results, they were very sympathetic and truly sad. I remember the look on my dad's face to this day. His eyes looked as though I had just told him that someone he loved had died—it was grief, pure and simple. I thought he might cry. But he sat and listened to all I had to say. After that he listened to the conversation between me and my mom. After a while, he seemed to gather strength and then he rose and told me that he wasn't worried about A because "he's a smart boy." I agreed but explained that his difficulties with understanding social and verbal communication might cause him troubles in the world. He just shook his head and said, "He is a good boy." I saw the denial at the same time I saw his understanding and his heartbreak. (Parent of A)

Grandparents can have as difficult a time accepting the diagnosis as parents do. Because they have less contact with the child, acceptance can take longer. The bonding process that helps parents learn to see the child instead of the disability is not always possible for grandparents. Grandparents who live far away and don't see their grandchild often may simply think that the child is fine and actually may be critical of the parent's decision to seek a diagnosis. They may feel defeated by the diagnosis and believe all attempts at intervention will be futile. Sometimes grandparents just get angry because they are overcome with fear and distress about their beloved grandchild (O'Brien and Daggett 2006).

Grandparents worry about their grandchild. They're watching the child and the family struggle. They may despair because they couldn't protect their child or their grandchild from the pain they are going through. This grandparent of a child with autism describes her concerns for the parents:

I worry about the marriage, about money, about their home, about their future. (O'Machel 2011, p.1)

Grandparents may be feeling overwhelmed with what they don't know and all the confusing information they may be reading or seeing on television about ASD. Grandparents are also often feeling guilty that they aren't able to help the family more. The grandparents may be too elderly, too ill, or too far away to offer the practical or emotional support they want to give.

Grandparents also have dreams for their grandchild that may have changed with the diagnosis. They, like parents, may be feeling grief over the loss of those dreams. The relationship the grandparents dreamed they would have with the grandchild may be changed because of difficulties interacting with the child. Their dreams of spending time with and caring for their grandchild may be changed because caring for the child is more complicated.

> I am sure there was a level of grief that my mother went through alone, that she hid from me as she offered me her unconditional love and support. It was particularly difficult for my mother at first because she was a very dedicated and involved Grandmother to my other two children. But my child who was ultimately diagnosed with autism would not have anything to do with her. I am sure in retrospect that it was hurtful before she understood. (Parent of B)

Grandparents can experience a kind of "triple grief." They are grieving for their child, grieving for their grandchild and grieving for themselves. They've lost the "typical" grandchild they were expecting and they are very worried about the stress in their child's life.

> The idea that grandparents grieve doubly (for their grandchild AND child) is very true, I believe, and my husband and I tried to be sensitive to the extra hurt they were feeling. It didn't feel like a burden to support them some in this way...it helped to ease the focus a bit. (Parent of A)

> The other side of it was [my father's] sadness and anger about my son basically looking right through him, not acknowledging his presence. He said to me, "You know what it's like to be ignored by your own grandson in your own house?" My mother was more attentive to our sadness and our frustration when we couldn't reach him. At one point near the end of our visit, she said to me, "We've been so caught up with how WE feel, we've forgotten how hard this must be for the two of you." I said I knew it was hard on all of us in different ways, and we both cried. (Parent of P)

Parents may be joining support groups and reading books and meeting other parents but grandparents typically have less access to support or information. They may have no way to work through their own grief (Baskin and Fawcett 2006). Finding other grandparents of children with ASD or meeting other families can be one way for grandparents to get the support they may need.

Grandparents, like other family members and friends, may not understand ASD and may not understand the behaviors the child may be having. How they react to the child and the situation may be a reflection of their confusion and misunderstanding about the disorder.

My mother-in-law told us that we shouldn't bring my son to family gatherings until he grows up. It's heart breaking to hear her say that she would rather not see any of us for years instead of trying to understand her own grandson. (Stone and DiGeronimo 2006, pp.94–95)

It is especially important to educate grandparents about the nature of ASD. When the grandparents were raising children, the "invisible" disorders like autism or learning disabilities were around but not understood or diagnosed. Understanding ASD can not only help with the grandparents' acceptance of the diagnosis but also help provide the understanding the grandparents will need to interact with their grandchild. The more that grandparents know, the more comfortable they will feel with the child.

It can be helpful to invite the grandparents to therapy sessions, doctor's appointments, or the child's school. Therapists and doctors generally welcome the presence of extended family members. The professional may even be willing to talk to the grandparents and answer questions they may have. It can be very educational for the grandparent to see their grandchild with other children or see them working on goals with the therapist. Helping parents transport the child to therapies or school can be a great way for grandparents to show support. Attending appointments may not only help educate the grandparents but also help them feel more involved.

Our daughter has two autistic sons. I have found that going to the therapy has really helped in understanding what is going on in these little boys. I was living in the next state and found it hard to make all of the sessions, but going to the ones I could helped not only myself, my daughter, but also brought me closer to my grandson. (Rudy 2009b, p.1)

Most grandparents don't have the intimate perspective and the experience that parents have living every day with the child with ASD. They also don't have training in behavior management and they may not physically be able to manage the behaviors of their grandchild with ASD. Parents should be aware of these limitations and help grandparents understand the behaviors when they happen and how to respond to them.

My father always wanted us to "give in" to my son's demands. It did and still does bother him immensely to see my son have a meltdown. Lots of times he would take it out on me. (Parent of E)

Parents need to continually educate grandparents and other family members and friends about any new issues the child may be having. If the child has specific behaviors that are problematic, family members and friends need to know what strategies might help. It is important for parents to talk to anyone who spends time with the child about how to redirect the child and about any reward systems they might be using. The strategies of spanking and scolding used in the past are not effective for children with ASD because of their limited ability to link consequences with their behavior or to think through the effect of their behavior on others (O'Brien and Daggett 2006). Grandparents and others will benefit from knowing how best to interact with the child.

Many grandparents are concerned with how to get to know their grandchild. They worry about how to approach the child and how to help them feel comfortable when they come to visit the grandparents' home. The parents can help with these concerns and should appreciate being asked about how to interact with their child. They also want their child and the grandparents to have a good relationship. Grandparents can ask about specific foods the child likes, activities they like, or things the child may need around them to feel comfortable. Change is hard for most children with ASD and having special items with them that are familiar can be helpful in a new environment. At the beginning grandparents may need to keep routines familiar, but over time as they get comfortable with each other new routines and unique ways to be together will develop (Rudy 2010).

Grandparents may have wisdom and experience from their own lives that can help the parents cope with this experience. In some situations, the grandparent may have training or experience with special needs. Their experience can be helpful to the family but the grandparent may struggle with how to balance the role they play. Dan, a psychologist and grandfather to Sam, describes:

> I struggled when I first noticed there was something wrong with Sam. He didn't seem to be hearing. I didn't know if he wasn't hearing or wasn't listening. Should I be at that point the father she depended on; the father with psychological training? Or should I be at that point the father who was supportive and had faith in her maternal instincts? My struggle with these issues goes on every time we are together. If I open my mouth, am I being controlling? If I keep my mouth shut, am I denying her some advice that might be helpful? (Ariel and Naseef 2006, p.129)

Grandparents can offer different ideas, opinions and perspectives that can oftentimes help the parents raising the child with ASD. Grandparents can also bring unique experiences to their grandchild with ASD.

> Grandpa spent a lot of time with my son, bringing him out in social situations (e.g. my son was obsessed with tall buildings

when he was young, and grandpa would take him to countless tall buildings, often hotels). One in particular had a piano on the top floor, and grandpa would have him play piano, usually for an audience. My son learned to speak up and initiate more (I believe) because of the experiences of being with his grandpa who is very outgoing and charismatic. I attribute a lot of my son's confidence these days to the early experiences that grandpa gave him. (Parent of A)

There are probably many words of wisdom that grandparents might have for the parents. Offering new parents advice is something most grandparents are guilty of; grandparents of grandchildren with disabilities are no exception. However, grandparents and other family members and friends should be careful about offering too much advice to the parents. Giving opinions or advice when the parents ask for it can be very helpful. Offering advice about how to parent a child with ASD when not requested by the parents may not be helpful.

Early on we bumped heads. I was trying to give advice, articles I had read, information on treatments people had told me about. Now I try to be supportive of their ideas (for their child). You will not be there to see those ideas through on a day-to-day basis. You are not walking in their shoes. (O'Machel 2011, p.2)

When grandparents are accepting and want to help, they can provide a valuable support system for the family. But they may struggle with finding their place with the adult children—where they fit in and how they can help. They may want to help financially. They may be able to help with locating information and services. They can provide much needed respite for the parents. Grandparents can also play an important role with other extended family members by serving as "information central" for answering questions and sharing information about the child (O'Brien and Daggett 2006).

Sometimes the best thing for grandparents to offer is to just be the parents' support system.

> We followed their lead and just made ourselves available. Sometimes we had to simply ask what specific thing we could do and when. (O'Machel 2011, p.2)

Grandparents can also play an important role in helping the siblings of the child with ASD. Parents are often so overwhelmed with the responsibilities of taking care of the child with ASD that they have less time to focus on the siblings. A grandparent's extra attention to the child who does not have autism serves to remind them of their importance in the family and how much they are loved.

However, it is also easy for grandparents, like parents, to become so focused on the child with the disability that they give much less attention to the other children in the family. It is important that the siblings also feel loved and appreciated by the grandparents.

> One negative was that my daughter (and my son with ASD's younger sibling) did not get the same level of attention and didn't have the same kind of bonding experience that my son got with his grandparents. Therefore, I've always felt this need to do extra esteem-building for my daughter, felt I was always compensating for what could be perceived, to a degree, as favoritism. (Parent of F)

When grandparents are perceived as supportive and non-judgmental there is typically greater cooperation between them and their adult child. A factor in building that trust between the parents and the grandparents is the genuine warmth and love the grandparents show for their grandchild.

> We're very fond of this kid... We don't think of him as disabled. We think of him as a person with a disability. (Katz and Kessel 2002, p.123)

So in summary, here are some things that grandparents can do to help themselves and to help the family.

Permit yourself time to grieve

You have suffered a loss too and it's okay to feel sad.

Seek current and accurate information about ASD

The more you understand about ASD, the more you will understand your grandchild.

Find support groups and opportunities to be with others who have ASD in their lives

Get involved with autism awareness activities in your community. Meeting other families and learning more about ASD will help you feel less alone.

Be a good listener to the child's parents

This may be the most important thing you can do to help the family.

Communicate your feelings without being judgmental or trying to take over

It's okay to ask questions and share your concerns. It's okay to share ideas, but respect the parents' decision about what is best for their child.

Let the parents know if you are uncomfortable interacting with your grandchild with ASD

It's okay to not know what to do. The parents didn't know what to do at first either. They will help you learn how best to interact with the child.

Reassure the parents that you are available if they need you

Hold to this offer and be available should they need you.

Get to know your grandchild and stay involved over time

Your relationship may be different than you expected, but it will be important in your life and your grandchild's life.

Give special attention to any siblings in the family

They need to feel special too.

Follow the rules set by the parents

Trust them to know what is right. Consistency is important for children with ASD.

If possible, offer respite

Parents need time away and someone they trust to look after their child (Brill 1994).

FRIENDS AND FRIENDSHIPS

Friendships can make a huge difference in a parent's ability to cope. Every parent needs someone to occasionally tell them that they are doing a good job, to listen to them when they need to talk, or just to help them feel less alone. In addition to encouragement, sometimes parents need their friends to be honest; someone to tell them when they are being unreasonable or unrealistic. Occasionally friends can also distract parents from their stressful lives and provide them with the opportunity just to be themselves. Friendships can be affected when a child is diagnosed with ASD (Morrell and Palmer 2006).

> Our social life naturally slowed down after having a child... but I just took him with us at first. Gradually, it got harder and harder to take him with us. My husband and I took turns socializing with our various friends, with one of us staying home with our child. (Parent of J)

> Our socializing didn't necessarily decrease much, but it changed because everything was more complicated and stressful. If we went to a park, he would cling to us instead of going on things and playing. If we went to someone's house with him, we had to constantly be on guard because his behavior was so erratic. (Parent of P)

In the study done by the Interactive Autism Network, when it came to friendships and social networks, nearly 60 percent of mothers and fathers reported that having a child with ASD had a negative impact overall. Parents also described significant strain on their friendships (Diamont 2010). Being a friend to someone during good times is easy. During the difficult times is when we learn who our true friends are. There are many reasons why friendships can be strained when a child is diagnosed with ASD. The parents are often so overwhelmed with helping their child that they don't have time to give to maintaining friendships.

> With friends who came after Justin, the test of whether the friendship would last was largely a matter of energy. If the friendship needed lots of time and attention, it was likely the relationship needed more than I was able to give it. The friendships that continued were the flexible and

low-maintenance ones. These friendships could accommodate my periods of self-absorption, unreturned phone calls, missed appointments, and the emotional roller-coaster ride that was my life. Luckily I kept many low-maintenance friendships and they enriched my life in indescribable ways. (Morrell and Palmer 2006, p.129)

There is frequently a sense of difference and a separation from the way life used to be that can interfere with continuing past relationships.

Life has changed, and often it is difficult for old friends to come along. (O'Brien and Daggett 2006, p.262)

Socially, we have fewer close friends. More friendships are flexible. Some of our very close friends and family too, for a time, almost dropped out of our lives. I think we have grown away from people too…our attitudes have changed. It makes us hard to be around. (Brower and Wright 1986, p.12)

As time has gone on I've become more polarized in my thinking and dealings with others when it comes to Jenny's autism. In spite of the progress, in spite of many people trying to understand, we will remain the odd family out. On the other hand, it makes it easier for me to stay focused on helping Jenny, and to be less concerned about how some of the decisions I have to make may impact others outside the family. (Ariel and Naseef 2006, p.38)

Socially, all of our friends changed initially, that is, we lost friends and acquired others. Our new friends tended to be people who had more than average concern and caring about social/human needs and rights. We sought out new friends who had common experiences and avoided, in particular, judgmental and biased people. (Brower and Wright 1986, p.14)

Parents may feel that friends who have neurotypical children can't relate to their situation and they can't relate to their friends' lives without ASD.

> After Jake was diagnosed, I had trouble trying to muster up feelings of joy upon hearing about a friend's daughter who sang in the school play or a friend's son who excelled at baseball, while my own son couldn't even speak, let alone hold a baseball bat. (Exkorn 2005, p.248)

> It was hurtful to hear about their children's "normal" lives and successes. They could have been more sensitive at times, yet, of course, I realize that they didn't mean to hurt me or make me feel bad. (Parent of J)

> Initially, right after the diagnosis, I had a hard time being out with my friends. If they complained about their children, I resented that. (Exkorn 2005, p.249)

Sometimes the differences between parents who have children with ASD and their friends who have neurotypical children do not become an issue that threatens the friendship.

> My friends with "typical" children will never understand my issues, but they are still friends. Sometimes it's nice to talk about normal kid issues, or not talk about kids at all. (Baskin and Fawcett 2006, p.47)

> We've maintained our friendships. My husband and I have always said that we wouldn't let our son's condition define us, so we actually don't purposely seek out other parents of autistic children. (Exkorn 2005, p.249)

One of my girlfriends once asked me if I wanted to hear about her child's successes. I knew then that I had failed my friend. If you are friends with a special needs mom, don't withhold sharing about your children. While there are times that your good news may feel unattainable to a special needs mom, she'll still want to share your joy. (Copeland 2011, pp.1–2)

I know it isn't exactly the same, but I love that my friends want to share their experiences with me, so I won't feel so bad. They support me as a parent and as a person, and they see my son for who he is—a kid with quirks who also has his strengths. (Exkorn 2005, p.250)

My friends who do not have children with a disability provide support from a different point of view, which is important to me as well. My longtime friend of 37 years does not know about autism or really much about disabilities in general except for what she knows from our relationship. When she spends time with my son I know she is not continually recognizing his autistic mannerisms (which I know is often natural for me and some of my friends who are more experienced with autism). When this friend sees my son, she sees more of the young man who is good, and wants to be enjoyed, loved, and helpful. Sometimes I feel that this friend, in some ways, sees my son closer to the way that I do. This reminds me to take a step back and appreciate and love my son in a more normal and less complicated way. (Parent of T)

In fact, friends who have children with ASD have much to offer their friends with neurotypical children. They can be a good shoulder to lean on when times get rough.

I've learned how to cope with many difficult times because I have "been there." So I can be empathetic and share my strength and support with my friends as they face their own challenges. (Baskin and Fawcett 2006, p.442)

As discussed in Chapter 3, sometimes friends may not know what to do or say to the parent of the recently diagnosed child. It's hard for them to know how to help and how much to help because everyone reacts differently and grieves differently. Sometimes the best thing friends can do is to stand by if needed, and not try to fix or direct anything.

> Sometimes our most helpful friends are known by what they don't do. My closest friends did not try to fix my life by advising me not to worry. They didn't gloss over my struggles by sharing stories of how other people had it much worse. They didn't feel they needed to defend God, trying to explain away the mysteries of why innocent people like Justin suffer. In fact, my friends often helped me the most by not talking about autism at all. It somehow showed me their faith in my ability to cope. (Morrell and Palmer 2006, p.131)

> I was just trying to be supportive of anything they did and to be supportive of any concerns they had…and mainly just to be there for my friend because I knew I couldn't be of help to the child since I had no experience in dealing with autism. (Friend of a parent)

Many children with ASD have challenging behaviors. These behaviors can be disruptive or odd and are not easily understood. Friendships can be affected if the child has difficult behaviors.

> I have lost many friends—and opportunities for friendship—because of my son's behavior. People aren't much interested in being with my little family, and I have stopped reaching out, as the rejection is painful. (Baskin and Fawcett 2006, p.40)

> I was shocked when some of my very closest friends asked us not to come back and play because they did not want my son around their children. (Autism Speaks 2009, p.2)

Being open with friends about the child's challenges may help.

> I talk to all my friends about Kevin. I explain his problems and what we're doing in therapy so they don't have to wonder and feel like they shouldn't ask. I talk about things he can do well, and I bring him when we go out so they see he's just a boy like other boys. The friends who are good friends handle it just fine. The ones who can't handle it, I figure I don't need. (Simons 1987, p.21)

But it's not always easy for parents of children with ASD to open up to their friends about things that are especially painful. They don't want to seem like they are complaining and they don't want to burden others with their problems. However, everyone needs friends to share their innermost thoughts. Without that, parents can feel very isolated.

> My closest friend knew. She called me for days after the diagnosis. I just couldn't talk about it yet. (BabyCenter 2011)

> If we let them in on the really challenging stuff, will they be scared away? On the other hand, if you always put on the cheery, competent mother role, you can't really get close to people. (Baskin and Fawcett 2006, p.41)

> It was difficult to help my friends understand. It was a challenge to paint an accurate picture without making it sound like our son was horrible. (Parent of G)

I didn't tell people. I have simply found the consequences of telling to be too big. If it becomes obvious, like my child walking in circles hitting himself in the head, I will tell people who are nearby. But I just do not tell general friends. Frankly, we do not have tons of friends. We have a 16 yr. old and a 9 yr. old with this diagnosis and that has been a huge friend repellent. Things go much better when people do not know. (BabyCenter 2011)

At first I found it difficult to share what we were going through with my old friends who had typical children, so we really relied on the friendships we made in the support groups. Now we're more comfortable speaking with and spending time with our friends who have typical children. It's like we have two sets of friends. And they're all special. (Exkorn 2005, p.249)

Parents may tell friends about their lives but they may hold back the really tough things. And sometimes they tell friends about the tough things and friends don't appreciate the seriousness of what they are being told. I have a friend, also a parent of a son with ASD, who has written a book about her experiences. When I asked her about her friendships and how they were affected by the diagnosis she said:

I cannot tell you how many people came up to me (and these are people I thought of as friends—good friends, close friends) after the book was published who said they had "no idea" things were that bad. And they meant that sincerely. They really had no idea. And so it must be that I didn't let them in on any of this. Which baffles me, because I remember talking about it. (Parent of C)

Parents want their friends' understanding but not their pity. I remember when my friend found out about my son's autism. Every time she saw me she would ask how I was doing in a tone of voice that immediately made me think she pitied me. It made me uncomfortable and I just wanted things to be the same between us. Unfortunately, it never was.

My husband and I have pulled away from many friends because they were always using "that voice"—the one where they are constantly feeling sorry for you. (Baskin and Fawcett 2006, p.40)

Everyone treats you like it is a disease and he could die... they are so sorry. Sometimes it would really bug me the way most people would react. It was mostly ignorance. Everyone is scared of the unknown. (Parent of E)

I don't have many close friends and the friends that I do have I told them nothing. I think my way of thinking is probably not like a lot of folks but the way I look at it, I'd rather not have the "I'm so sorry" or the "woe is me" sympathy that I'm not looking for... Because in all actuality if you've never gone through it personally, there's no way they can understand what it is like on a day-to-day basis. Plus to be honest, I just really didn't feel like explaining it all. (BabyCenter 2011)

Friendships naturally go through phases where the proportions of giving and receiving support fluctuate. Overall there should be a reciprocal balance of give and take in a friendship (Marshak and Prezant 2007). For parents of children with ASD, they may feel like they need too much support and have limited opportunities to return the support to their friend who doesn't have a child with ASD. In those cases, the parent may need to make a conscious effort to regularly ask their friend if there is something they can do for them.

I have friends, who do not know much about how our lives are when you have a child with a disability, who could not be more caring and supportive. With these friends it is easy to have a

> more balanced relationship where both sides talk and listen to each other and autism is not always the dominant topic. (Parent of T)

Parents of children with ASD often have difficulties in building and maintaining friendships with those friends who do not understand ASD well. Maybe that is why so many parents reach out to other parents of children with ASD who are more understanding of the difficulties the family is facing. That network of support can not only provide information about resources in the community, but can also serve to connect parents who have similar children and similar struggles.

> This has been the greatest support of my life. When I occasionally feel sorry for myself and think about the lack of involvement and support I received from my family, I turn to the gift of support and love I've gotten from my "autism" friends. It more than makes up for anything missing. My friends with children with disabilities are my "rock." Not only do I get inspiration from them but I get the much needed respite from the world with them! (Parent of B)

> How do I describe my friendships with other moms of children with autism? These are the people who know the real me. These are the friends I call when Eric does something great or when Eric is struggling. We all understand that we aren't "Super Moms" simply because we have a child with a disability. We can be honest with each other about our self-doubts and the mistakes we make. These friends don't judge me or my choices. If I go to their homes with my family it's not stressful. I don't have to explain why Eric is only eating crackers and Cheerios and won't eat whatever the others are having. These are the friends who understand my life, and I understand theirs. (Morrell and Palmer 2006, p.130)

My friends who have a family member with a disability have been very helpful as far as support and sharing information about resources to help my son and my family and also in assisting me in building a network of more friends, acquaintances, and services in the "world of autism/disabilities." I have a few friends I have a special bond with—who are friends I can easily talk to because they understand what life is like when your child has a disability (even when your situation is different from theirs)... It is a relationship where we understand and respect each other's busy lives, successes, commitments, worries, and needs. There is true affection and extensive appreciation for these friends, even when you do not see each other or connect with each other on a frequent or even regular basis. We have a mutual understanding about how autism is a very large part of our lives. And we share a desire to work to help improve the lives of people with autism and their families. (Parent of T)

My friend network has become 90 percent parents of children with autism. There is no way to describe the support these families give to one another. Just knowing that there is a level of unconditional caring, support and acceptance is worth so much. (Parent of B)

Obviously, friendships are important to the parents living with a child with ASD. Friendships help keep the parents from feeling isolated and can offer the encouragement they need during difficult times. In the next chapter we will discuss how friends and family members can support the family living with ASD and how the parents can offer them the support they may need.

Chapter 5

SUPPORTING EACH OTHER

Support from family members and friends is crucial to the family living with ASD. When the parents are feeling supported, they are more likely to access services and treatments for their child and more likely to have good mental health and family well-being. Research has shown that support from grandparents, other members of the extended family, and from friends is more important to adaptation to a crisis than support from professionals (Sandler, Warren and Raver 1995). And for families of children with ASD, there may be a greater need for social or practical support from extended family and friends than is needed for other families without autism in their lives (Glasberg and Harris 1997).

There are many ways that extended family members and friends can show support to the family living with ASD. This chapter discusses some of the helpful ways to support a family, including ways to provide emotional support and ideas for practical support that can be offered to the family. In addition, it is important to discuss some of the mistakes people may make in their attempts to show their support. We discuss some of the things that may be said or done that ultimately cause more stress than help to the family living with ASD.

Support is a two-way street. The parents of the child with ASD also have an important role in helping to build a trusting, positive relationship with family members and friends. There are ways that parents can make it easier for others to understand their situation and easier for them to be supportive. People who care about the child and care about the parents are also grieving and may need support and understanding from the parents living with ASD.

> I didn't know what to say. I cried along with my friend. We talked and I tried to make her feel better, but I didn't know anything about autism or mental retardation. I guess I just listened, as good friends do, to all her concerns, etc. I tried to be positive when deep inside I was hurting. (Friend of a parent)

> I felt inadequate as a friend... I didn't know anything about autism and while I wanted to help, I felt completely at a loss to do so. (Friend of a parent)

WAYS FAMILY AND FRIENDS CAN SHOW SUPPORT

Family members and friends often do not automatically know what to do or say when told about the diagnosis.

> I think it was hard on some of my friends especially since I couldn't talk about it without crying. It's very similar to when someone gets diagnosed with cancer. No one knows what to say. (Parent of E)

> The on-the-spot news of this over the phone was very disturbing and surprising, I'm sure, and I'll only ever feel gratitude for the people in my family who tried to help in whatever way they could. No one ever gasped in shock or made me feel worse—truthfully, there was really nothing anyone could have said those first few weeks that would have made me feel less distressed. (Parent of A)

Sometimes the support that is needed the most is actual physical support where the family member or friend pitches in and helps. This kind of support could include activities such as helping to run errands, mowing the lawn, washing the clothes, or driving the child to therapies. Bringing an occasional meal for the family or helping with carpooling the kids to activities can free up much needed time for the parent to take a shower or a nap. There are always more things to do in a day than any parent can accomplish and having assistance with some of the daily responsibilities can be extremely helpful to parents.

Babysitting so the parents can go out together or watching the child with ASD for brief times during the day can be another helpful way to support the family. It not only allows the parents to get a break, but also lets the family member or friend get to know the child with ASD better. However, not all family members or friends will feel comfortable offering this kind of support.

> What do I wish they had done to help my family? In my dreams? Offered to keep him overnight or for a weekend...offering much needed respite...but I know they were uncomfortable and didn't feel they were able to. (Parent of J)

If you don't know the child well and don't know how his or her ASD affects them, you may be nervous about spending time with them alone. I would suggest that you first spend some time with the child and the parents together, getting to know the child's likes and dislikes and what strategies the parents use in interacting with the child. It's okay to let the parents know you are nervous about spending time with the child because you aren't sure what to do if the child should get upset. The parents should appreciate your honesty and with luck they will give you the information you need to feel more confident in providing this kind of support.

> Early on my parents came to stay with my three kids so we could go away for a weekend. This was the first time we had

EVER left our son with autism. I left about six pages of notes explaining how things had to be done a certain way, etc. Unfortunately, I forgot to mention that I NEVER let the water drain out of the bathtub until my son was in his room with a video on so he couldn't hear the noise. Well, my poor mom had a time trying to figure out why he got so very upset when she tried to drain the bathtub, but she worked through it. (Parent of B)

Not all parents will accept offers to babysit the child with ASD and they may not ask people to help with taking care of the child. If the child with ASD has challenging, unpredictable behaviors, the parents may not feel comfortable leaving them with someone. They may have concerns about the child's safety. They may not want to put that kind of burden on a family member or friend. It may just seem too difficult to "teach" someone else how to take care of their child.

My parents watched our kids on occasion when we needed help while our son was still small and they could manage him. As he grew and his behavior became more challenging, we did not ask family for help as we knew it was too much for them. (Parent of T)

My friend didn't want anyone but her and her husband or daughters to be with their son alone. They felt that we might not be prepared to take care of him if something went wrong. I can understand that so it didn't make me feel bad. (Friend of a parent)

If the family member or friend sees this kind of support as a critical need for the parents, it may be helpful to suggest that the parents consider a professional organization that can provide respite services to the family. Having trained professionals provide childcare may be more acceptable to the parents. The important thing is that the parents get a break now and then from their parenting responsibilities, whether it is provided by a family member or friend or a paid respite provider.

For those of you who live far away from the family with a child with ASD, you are probably struggling to know how to help. You can also "be there" for the family without actually physically being there. Calling regularly to see how things are going, sending a note that you are thinking of them, regularly asking if there is anything you can do to help, all will help the parents feel supported.

> I just wish they had called more to check in with me. (Parent of C)

You probably really want to help the family in some way but many parents feel uncomfortable asking for help from their family and friends. They may have difficulty verbalizing ways that you can help them. They may need your help but feel badly about having to ask.

> Though I hated to ask, my neighbors and friends were usually willing to help. When they went out to shop, they incorporated some of my errands with theirs. They also included [the siblings] with their kids for many of their after-school and weekend activities. (Morrell and Palmer 2006, p.118)

If you really want to help the family, you may need to ask the parents how you can help.

> I wish they had asked how they might help, how best to support us, to approach him. (Parent of P)

If the parents initially can't suggest ways they can be helped, keep asking. If they are not able to give ideas about how you can help, you may need to suggest things you can do. Suggest errands you can run, meals you can bring, or babysitting you can provide. You may find that parents are more able to ask for help or suggest ways to help as time goes on and they understand more about their limits and struggles and feel more comfortable asking for help.

Family members and friends may choose to help the family financially as a way to show their support. As was discussed earlier, it is very expensive to raise a child with ASD and most families can use financial help. You will first have to decide if it is appropriate to offer the parents money and whether the parents will be comfortable with that kind of offer. You don't want the parents to feel that your offer to help financially means you believe they are not providing adequately for the child. Ideas of financial support might include offering to pay toward a therapy the child is receiving, paying for a week at camp for the child, buying something the family needs for the child in the home, giving the parents a gift certificate to a bookstore that sells books on autism or to a restaurant for a night out. Another way to show your support financially is to participate in walks for autism or other kinds of fundraising. Family members and friends can show their support by making a donation in honor of the child to a non-profit agency that supports individuals with ASD or by making a donation to a particular program that is helping the child.

> We had a full "coming out" if you will when we did an Autism Speaks walk last fall. We sent out an email to friends and family—whether they already knew of DD's diagnosis or not. And the overwhelming generosity and support rocked our world. (BabyCenter 2011)

One of the most helpful ways to support the family may be the easiest—the simple act of listening. It is often not the great deeds that are done for the family that bring the most comfort. It is the sensitivity the family member or friend shows and their understanding that the parents are hurting. Sometimes no words are needed.

The most helpful thing someone did for me was listen to my feelings. (Brower and Wright 1986, p.10)

A friend brought lunch to my home on a day that I learned the self-contained classroom my daughter was to be placed in had no room for her. My friend let me cry and be sad, but she was there, and I knew someone cared. (Brower and Wright 1986, p.9)

Giving the parent the opportunity to talk about what they are going through is incredibly important. Listening, without judging, makes the parents feel supported and less alone. Touching base with them regularly to see how things are going lets the parents know you care and you are thinking of them. Asking questions can encourage the parents to talk and to share their hopes and concerns.

What do I wish they had done to help my family? I wished they had asked more questions and asked about the resources we searched for when we moved to an area we thought would help us. I wished they had asked about B's school program and as he got older, asked us what our dreams for B were when he became an adult. (Parent of B)

What did our friends do to offer their support? Mostly just acknowledging the difference and asking questions. This is so much better than ignoring or pretending it doesn't exist! This shows true interest in our child. (Parent of B)

You may not have all the answers; you won't be able to "fix" the problem, but that's okay. Telling the parent that you know this is difficult, that you support their decisions, that you know they are doing what is best for their child, is very powerful and very supportive.

Validating the parents' feelings and understanding how hard this is for them is a wonderful first step.

> My mother once said to me, "I don't understand what you are living with, but I trust you and know you are doing the best you can." This not only validated me, but also allowed me to not be angry with my family as they really *didn't* understand. (Parent of B)

> I wish they had recognized right off how painful a discovery this was for us and how gently they needed to tread. (Parent of P)

> You can be a "friend" to parents of children with autism by supporting them unconditionally, forgiving them for forgetfulness, tardiness, or lack of free time. You can be their friend simply by listening or being there when needed, just like you know they would do for you. (Centamore 2009)

There are other simple ways to show the family your support that don't cost any money. Family members or friends can offer to make phone calls for the parents when they are researching schools or therapies. You can go online and research programs the parents are interested in and collect information to give them. You can offer to go with the parents to meetings that might be difficult, or go with them to observe classrooms or programs. You can serve as the "contact person" for other family members when updates or information needs to be disseminated to the family.

Friends and family members may want to show their support by sharing with the parents what they are seeing in magazines, TV, and newspapers about new treatments and research findings for ASD. This can be helpful in moderation. Constantly getting articles about autism treatments may make the parents believe that you think they are not doing enough for their child or are not making the right decisions about treatment options. It's also important to realize that parents don't always agree about autism treatments or theories of potential causes of autism. They may have strong reactions to information you send them. It is best if you talk to the parents first and see if they would like you to send them the information you've found.

Showing interest and asking about the child with ASD and their progress is another way to show your support. All parents like to talk about their children and parents of children with ASD are no exception. Asking how the child is doing gives the parents an opening to talk more about their child with someone else, and that can be very helpful. You may not be able to physically be with the child regularly but you can still stay involved by understanding the child and appreciating their challenges and strengths.

Getting to know the child with ASD and showing your love of the child is a wonderful way to show your support. You'd be surprised by the number of parents who report that people ignore their child, don't ask about the child, and pretend like the child does not exist. Showing interest in the child with ASD and finding ways to interact with them shows the parents that you accept the child for who they are.

Over the years my parents came to love B very much and showed that when they visited. This was more important to me than hearing advice or getting actual support from them. (Parent of B)

My friends stayed in touch, continued to be our friends and asked how things were going with our son's progress. They also asked about our other children and other things in our lives, as would be usual with your friends. When any of my friends come to see me and they visit with T, they give him sincere attention. For me, when my friends support and enjoy my son, I feel supported, too. (Parent of T)

Getting to know the child with ASD also helps the family member or friend better understand the challenges the family may be facing every day.

> When we did visit and her son was there, it made us understand even more how difficult it was to have a child with a disability. It took all their attention. They love him very much, but you could tell that it was very, very tiring. (Friend of a parent)

Finding out what the child enjoys and what their strengths are can also help in developing ways to connect to the child.

> Some family members still don't get who our son is. They buy him baseball gloves, bats, ball when all he wants to do is stand and watch trains. He can no more catch a ball than he can catch the moon. But they feel that buying him "normal" things will make him "normal." (Marshak and Prezant 2007, p.188)

You can also share in the accomplishments of the child with ASD. Parents will feel very supported when their family member or friend celebrates the child's improvement or accomplishments with them, no matter how small they may seem. Part of adjusting to living with ASD is learning to take things step by step and celebrating the small things, any achievement the child accomplishes. Being able to share those times will mean a great deal to the parent and will strengthen your relationship with them.

Another way to show support is by including the child with ASD in social events and outings. As we have discussed, it can be very painful for parents when their child is excluded from birthday parties or events.

> They didn't invite him to family functions at their house. They always asked if I could find a sitter. (Parent of D)

Over time, we were no longer invited to the birthday parties and cookouts, although these were not my true friends. They might have been if my child were just like theirs. (Parent of B)

Although it may be difficult in many ways for the family to attend these kinds of events, the parents need to know their family and child are included and wanted. Don't assume they won't or can't attend an event and not invite them. Allow the family to decide if the child can handle being there or not. If you have children, invite the child with ASD over for a play date. For the child with ASD it will give them the opportunity to work on social skills with other children. For the neurotypical child it can provide a lesson in acceptance of people who may be different.

Getting together with family and good friends is usually a very important part of life for most people. Celebrating holidays and events is a way that families stay connected and feel supported. But family get-togethers, holiday gatherings or large social events are typically very stressful for a family with a child with ASD. The child with ASD may not function well in large, loud crowds. Going to a new place with new people and no way to predict what will happen can be a nightmare for a child with ASD.

These kinds of events can be a nightmare for the parents as well. Parents often find themselves being the "buffer" for their child; trying to prevent them from doing or saying the wrong thing, having to watch the child constantly to make sure they don't run off, worrying about whether the child will get upset. This can be very exhausting.

I could barely carry on a conversation with anyone for having to chase my child all over the house to prevent disaster from occurring. (Autism Speaks 2009, p.3)

If there are people at the event who the parents haven't seen in a while, they may be faced with uncomfortable questions about their child or have to talk about the diagnosis. This can be stressful as well.

Parents also may feel sad watching other children playing together, reminding them of their child's differences and isolation. For these reasons families sometimes make the painful decision to stop going to family functions because they are so difficult. This can add to their feelings of isolation.

> Our relationship [with our family] has suffered because we are out of circulation and have neglected extended family functions. (Autism Speaks 2009, p.3)

There are ways to make the child and the family feel more comfortable at family gatherings and parties. First of all, make sure the family knows that you want them there and you are willing to help in any way you can. Ask them how you can make the day better for them. Ask the family what foods the child likes to eat, or if the child is on a special diet, what foods they are allowed to eat. Make sure some of them are available. Suggest the parents bring any items with them that would help the child feel more comfortable such as books, toys or videos. Arrange a place in the house where the child can go if he or she gets overwhelmed and needs to be in a quiet place. If possible, offer to spend some time with the child at the party so the parents can socialize with others. Don't insist that the child sit at the dinner table with others or participate in games, gift opening, etc. These activities may be too difficult for the child with ASD.

> Probably the most important thing that my family does, or doesn't do, is judge. At holidays when my son was younger and just couldn't handle the crowd, no one mentioned it. When he sits at the Thanksgiving table now and needs ketchup to dip his turkey in and doesn't eat anything green, that's okay! There has been a real feeling of acceptance and understanding for my son and for our parenting. This is a blessing! (Parent of B)

The key to being supportive in this kind of situation is to be understanding, flexible, and accepting. If the family has to leave early, or decides not to attend at all, understand that the parents know their child's limits. Don't take it personally. Knowing that you invited them and knowing that you are willing to do everything you can to make it possible for them to be there is a wonderful way to show your support.

Parents of the child with ASD can also do things to make family gatherings and parties with friends more successful. Sharing information about the child with those who are going to be there may be helpful. It might help to tell others about the difficulties your child may have talking to people they don't know or tolerating loud places and large crowds. Let them know that you are working with your child to help them adapt to these kinds of situations, but it is still difficult and you appreciate their understanding. Parents can also help by preparing the child with ASD as much as possible beforehand. Help them understand where they are going, who will be there, and how long they will be there. If possible, explain what they might be doing while they will be there. Children with ASD are typically stressed by the unknown, so communicating the expectations of the day can be very helpful.

If friends find it is too difficult to get together with the child and the family in a larger social setting, they could invite the family over without other guests. This can be more casual and more comfortable for the child. The goal is to make sure the family doesn't feel isolated and to remind them that people care about them and their child. Bringing over your children to play at the home of the child with ASD is another way to support the family. This may be easier for the family because the child will be in an environment where they are comfortable and not somewhere new. Parents will appreciate every opportunity to have their child meet another child and perhaps develop a friendship.

My friends were surprised about the diagnosis but have been my saving grace. They bring their kids over for play dates and give our son special attention. (Exkorn 2005, p.249)

What did I do to help friends understand what was going on with my child? I invited them over to my house. If they could handle a visit, then they could stay my friend. (Parent of E)

It is often equally important to spend time with the siblings of the child with ASD. They can easily get "lost in the shuffle" and usually love having special time with their family members or friends without their sibling with ASD. Parents may be worried about the lack of time they have available to focus on the siblings and invitations to activities by friends and family can help.

My BFF (Best Friend Forever) called last night to see if our older son (our son without autism) wanted to go on a little trip with her family in May. She said Holden needs special attention too. (BabyCenter 2011)

As you can see, there are many ways you can help the family and show your support. Remember that the need for support is not only during the initial time after receiving the diagnosis. That is an important time for family members and friends to reach out to help the family, but parents will need the support of their family and friends throughout their lives with the child with ASD. Oftentimes people stop offering help because time has passed and they assume the parents have adapted.

To family and others, we seem okay, because we have done it for so long. (Baskin and Fawcett 2006, p.266)

The reality is that the parents will continue to struggle at times and can use the support of their family and friends. Adolescence and adulthood will bring new stresses and concerns and support is still crucial for the family.

> I could tell just by the tone of her voice that she was stressed, even though she didn't admit it. When her son was older and they were trying to find the best place for him to live, that whole ordeal was very, very stressful and that, I have to say, was the lowest and the most stressed I have ever heard my friend be. I could tell she was at the end of her rope. After going back and forth between group homes and finally finding the home that was good for her son and giving him the services that he so desperately needed, she and her family finally could relax and feel happy again. (Friend of a parent)

In summary, there are many ways an extended family member or friend can be supportive to the family, immediately following the diagnosis and over time. This quote from the sister of Gina, who just found out about her child's diagnosis, describes a good example of a supportive relationship all parents would like to have:

> How did I help Gina? I asked her to talk. I listened to her. I asked her many questions. I did not give her advice or lectures. I validated her anger, fears, and frustrations. I felt honest compassion for her. I did not feel "sorry" for her. I did not get upset over her dilemma or judge her. I was not impatient. I believed deep down she knew exactly what she needed to do, and my only job was to let her talk until she could come up with her own solutions. You could say I was a safe person for Gina. (Gallagher and Konjoian 2010, p.54)

Gina Gallagher and Patricia Konjoian in their book, *Shut Up about Your Perfect Kid: A Survival Guide for Ordinary Parents of Special Children* (2010), describe their definition of a "safe" person as someone who allows you to be confused and crazy and doesn't want to "fix" you. A safe person is clear and honest with the parent and has no personal agendas; they just want to be compassionate and validate the parent's feelings. This sounds like the perfect kind of support for parents of children with ASD; unfortunately sometimes those we may love the most may not be the "safest" people during a crisis (Gallagher and Konjoian 2010).

ATTEMPTS TO SUPPORT THAT DON'T HELP

The extended family member or friend may have great empathy for what their loved one is going through but still end up saying or doing something that may be hurtful. At a stressful time we may not always know the perfect thing to say or do. Our instincts may be to say what we think the parents want to hear, but that may not be as helpful as we think.

For example, reminding the parent how bad it is may not be very helpful. Most parents do not want to be singled out as martyrs. They don't want to be considered "special" just because they have a child with ASD (Brower and Wright 1986). They are just ordinary parents who are facing difficult circumstances. People may say, "I couldn't do what you do." Or they may say, "You must be very special for God to have chosen you to have a 'special' child." These kinds of comments don't typically make the parent feel better. It can make parents believe you think that they deserved this fate somehow, or that you think this situation hurts them less than it would hurt you. The parent most likely is not feeling strong or "special" and does not think they are doing a good job at all. These kinds of comments may only make parents feel like more of a failure. Statements like "God doesn't give you more than you can handle" can also add to the stress the parent is already feeling. Most likely the parent is feeling like they are barely surviving and this kind of statement may only convince them that they should be able to handle it better.

I remember one of my immediate family members saying something about how God couldn't have chosen two people better than us to parent a child with autism, almost as if we were "chosen." In hindsight, I'm not sure that this was helpful...but I think it was their way of trying to make a sad situation more positive. (Parent of A)

I actually hated hearing how lucky J was to have us as parents...irrationally, I felt responsible somehow and wished that he'd been born to someone else if that would have saved him from this diagnosis. In no way could I accept that he was "lucky," and I found that sentiment particularly offensive, though I knew it was well-meaning. (Parent of J)

Several of [our friends] credited our being so involved and so dedicated to account for his being very high functioning. That was comforting, but we always felt guilty for not having been as patient and as creative as necessary. (Parent of P)

It also doesn't help when a family member or friend tells the parents that it could be worse. First, the parents probably are seeing their experience as very painful and difficult, and are not comparing their experience with the experiences of others. Second, reminding them that it could be worse may only add to the worries they already have about additional difficulties the child may have in the future. Third, if someone tells a parent it could be worse, they may feel guilty that people perceive them as complainers. This may encourage them to keep their true feelings hidden from others.

Another dangerous thing to say to parents of a child with ASD is "I know just how you feel." You may have dealt with a very difficult experience yourself. You may have a child who has a disability or a serious medical condition. But most likely you don't know how that parent feels. Even if you are another parent with a child with ASD, every experience and every child with ASD is unique. Instead it is more helpful to say, "I know this must be very hard" or, "I wish I could say something to make it better but I don't know what that might be."

That is an honest response that opens up the dialogue for the parent to talk about what is hard and it tells them you are concerned and know they may be struggling.

Family members and friends may at times say, "All children do that" or, "My child did that too and I responded this way…" Yes, the child with ASD may be having difficulties that are common to others, but it is the degree and extent of the difficulty in that child's life that often makes it very different.

> When I began explaining what the diagnosis meant in [my son's] situation my brother agreed that his boys did similar things—even though they were several years younger. I suppose it was his attempt at comforting me. I found it irritating. I always hated it when people would tell me that their child was like A—which was not at all true. (Parent of A)

Chances are the parents are confused about whether their child's behaviors are caused by the ASD or not, and they are struggling to figure out what strategies to use to help with the behaviors. Reminding parents of what strategies work with neurotypical kids will probably not be helpful since those strategies usually do not work with children with ASD.

One mistake that is often made is for family members and friends to give the parents unsolicited advice. It is human nature to want to share our opinion, and if you love the child and the parents, you may feel compelled to try to help them by giving advice. It is important to remind ourselves that the parents are living this 24/7. They know their child better than anyone else can.

> I remember one time when one of those wacky treatments came out, injections of serotonin or something, and one of my sisters called me and said I needed to get my son some of that… It was the way she approached it, like fix him, make him normal. I don't know, but I remember being really pissed off! (Parent of E)

I remember one "friend" who I was very close to who made a comment about the fact that he was just different from his other brothers and that he should not be labeled. It was just a general feeling of non-support. Well, we are not friends anymore. (Parent of B)

Some [of our friends] who had a few children of their own ("experienced" parents) tried to give us advice based on things they did with their own kids and usually didn't understand that it wasn't the same, that everything was a lot harder for us. It wasn't hurtful—just annoying. (Parent of P)

When someone gives advice about how to help with a particular behavior problem, for example, it only serves to make the parent feel worse. They have probably tried your suggestion or know for a fact that it will not work because of their knowledge about their child and about ASD. Wait until the parent asks for your opinion and advice. That is when it is most helpful. This parent's comments explain it well:

People looking in from the outside—grandparents, aunts and uncles, classmates' parents—they think they have some advice for you. They think they have an answer you haven't found, because they were successful with their kids and you aren't. It's like people without kids giving advice about kids, only worse, because I know that their experience was nothing like mine in raising her. I always feel that the subtext is that she would be more normal if only we did this or that. (Klass and Costello 2003, p.140)

The unsolicited advice that most often triggers negative reaction from parents, mothers in particular, are comments about the child's eating habits or toilet training. Both of these topics are very sensitive issues for parents. Mothers, who typically have the primary responsibility of feeding their child and making sure they become toilet trained, are often very stressed over these two particular issues. Comments or questions about the child who is not toilet trained yet or the unusual eating habits of the child can bring up some strong emotions.

As mentioned in Chapter 1, children with ASD often have sensory issues that affect what they can eat. They may eat only a few kinds of foods and these foods often have to be prepared a certain way, or be a certain brand, or come from a particular restaurant. Substitutions don't work. The child with ASD can often notice very slight changes in foods. And trying new foods is next to impossible. For the parent, this is an incredibly challenging issue and one that mothers can take very personally.

Our roles as mothers include making sure our children are healthy and eating properly. Having a picky eater challenges a mother's ability to be a good parent. The strategies that parents use to encourage kids to try new foods often do not work for children with ASD. Children with ASD can outlast any patient parent who won't let the child leave the table until they eat their green beans. I personally struggled with this. My son was a very picky eater and I tried everything to get him to broaden the number of foods he would eat, to no avail. Mealtime became an ongoing battle and was very stressful. So when my mother-in-law would make offhand comments like, "Does he eat anything green at all?" it would feel like a reminder of my failure at being a good mother to my son.

One parent talks about her choice to prioritize what is most important:

> With everything else involved in raising an autistic child, I tend to give the least emphasis to his diet. I figure a lot of normal kids survive on rotten diets and I have only so many hours in a day. There's just no time to force-feed Lawrence every meal. (Powers 1989, p.101)

Potty training a child with ASD can also be extremely difficult. Difficulties with communication, sensory issues, fears, and insistence on routines, can all interfere with a parent's ability to toilet train their child. As with picky eating issues, typical strategies families may use for toilet training often do not work for children with ASD. Family members and friends do not need to remind the parent that the child needs to be toilet trained by the time they go to kindergarten. Believe me, the parent knows and is stressed about it.

> My mother-in-law questioned our methods. She could not understand why my son was not potty trained and kept telling us what to do. She was very critical. (Parent of E)

Family members or friends may also at times think that the parent is being overreactive or overprotective and subsequently make comments or give advice that are not helpful. For example they may not understand why a parent may remove a child from a situation or why they won't let their child try new things. In these situations parents are typically reacting based on information they have about their child that others might not. They know when to remove their child from a situation because they are sensitive to the cues their child gives indicating increased agitation or stress. They have learned how to predict the kinds of events that will lead to problems for their child (O'Brien and Daggett 2006). Trust the parents to know their child's limits and avoid commenting if possible.

As mentioned in Chapter 4, family members or friends may withdraw from the child or from the family. That can happen because they don't know what to do or say and they are uncomfortable around the child. I have to believe that most people who withdraw don't understand how hurtful this is to the family. The parents can help by talking about it with the person who is withdrawing and letting them know they miss their involvement in their lives. They may need to educate the family member or friend about ASD or give them strategies to have successful interactions with the child. Giving them something to read or inviting them to support group meetings might help. Confronting them about what is happening may be difficult, but if the parents want to continue the relationship, it may be necessary to have this conversation.

HOW PARENTS CAN SUPPORT FRIENDS AND FAMILY

If you are a parent of a child with ASD, take some time now to think about your relationship with your extended family and with your friends and the kind of support system you currently have. Is there anything you can do to strengthen those relationships? In Chapter 4 we discussed some of the obstacles that can get in the way of a positive supportive relationship between the parents of children with ASD and their extended family and friends. One of these obstacles can be the parents' unwillingness to tell others about their child's difficulties.

Despite the difficulty of telling others, parents need to be open about the diagnosis and about their feelings and what they are going through. It is important to be honest; you did nothing wrong and you have nothing to hide (Brill 1994).

A lot of times my friend would talk about how hard it was at times to deal with her son and his behavioral issues, but she always made it sound as if it was OK. I wish that she would have told me about some of the challenges that she faced because it would have made me understand more of what she was actually going through... It wouldn't make me love her son less, I would have understood more about his autism and why he did what he did. I guess I'm not saying that she didn't talk to me about her feelings, because she did, but I feel a lot of times she tried to "sugar coat" it, as if it wasn't as bad as it really was. "Everything is OK" she would say time and time again when I knew deep down it wasn't. (Friend of a parent)

You may fear the judgments and reactions of others when you tell them the news...and indeed you may not get the response you hope for from everyone you love. But support from a close circle of family and friends is one of the most important resources parents of children with special needs can have, and people can't support you if you don't give them a chance. (Mauro 2011)

The best way to build a good support system is to help family and friends learn about your child's ASD. Talk with immediate family members as soon as possible. Focus on the child's strengths and remind them that the ASD is only one part of who they are.

> If you want your family and friends to be optimistic, you have to lead the way. If you want them to see your child as a total child, you have to be their guide. If you want them to focus on your child's progress, so must you... And remember nobody's perfect—not even your family and friends. (Miller 2002, p.209)

> The family couldn't be more awesome...they support their child in every way they can and they allow their friends to interact with him and include us in his triumphs and joys. (Friend of a parent)

Tailor what you say and how you say it to the person you are telling, depending on how close they are to you or the child. Sometimes the person will only need a minimal amount of information and others closer to the family may need more. You don't want to bombard them with too much information and overwhelm or confuse them. Share information on a need-to-know basis.

> Our family received a newsletter that helped us to understand more. The newsletter spurred my interest to read more about autism. As an aunt, I wanted to know what was going on in someone's brain who is autistic, so that I could know how to act around my nephew. I didn't want to be surprised by aspects of his behavior, and I wanted to be one of the people who could take some burden off his parents if they needed me to help out in any way. (Aunt of R)

Parents should consider giving family members and friends a short list of internet sites so that they can look at information about ASD at their own pace. Family and friends should be encouraged to ask questions and share their concerns. It was confusing and overwhelming to parents when they were first learning about ASD. It is the same for relatives and friends. It may be difficult at first, but talking about the child's ASD will get easier for the parents with time and experience.

Educating your friends about ASD should also include educating them about your particular child with ASD. Family and friends need to understand how the disorder affects their loved one.

> I tried to help them understand that he had a behavior disorder, not bad behavior. I also explained to them that he didn't like to be touched. They thought physical affection would help. (Parent of D)

Family and friends will be better supports to you and develop more meaningful relationships with the child if they feel comfortable around the child and understand some of the behaviors they may see. Parents can plan times when the family member or friend can spend time with the child to get to know them better.

> I tried to share as much information as possible. I also exposed my child to my family as much as possible; thinking the more time they spent around him, the more they would understand. (Parent of E)

Parents can suggest practical methods for interacting with the child and suggest what kinds of toys, videos, etc. would appeal to them. The more the parents educate the family and friends, the less surprises or disappointments. Parents may also need to re-educate others as time goes by. There will be new people joining the family, cousins get older and may need to be educated as they are more able to understand, and the child with ASD will be changing over time and new information may need to be shared.

Some relatives or friends may never ask about the child or show any interest in how he or she is doing. One parent I know decided to tell folks about the child regularly, whether they asked about them or not. She assumed that people might not be asking about the child because they were uncomfortable or they didn't know what to ask. She would send out regular email updates about the child's progress and what the family was doing to help him. This can help people feel more involved and can help answer questions they may be having that are too difficult to ask.

Another way to help educate family members or friends is to invite them to the child's therapy appointments or to the school so they can see the progress he or she is making. If the parents are involved in a support group with other families of children with ASD, they can consider inviting family members or friends to attend. They will get a much clearer picture of what ASD is when they meet other families who are also living with this experience.

In addition to being open with others about the diagnosis and how it affects the child, parents also need to be open about their own feelings. Some family members and friends may be trying to protect you by hiding their true emotions. If the parents are open about their feelings, family members and friends will have their own feelings validated and may be more willing to talk about their concerns. This will help to build a more trusting relationship.

It is also important for parents to remember to be friends to their friends who don't live with autism. They have stresses in their lives too, and even though it is not the same as living with ASD, it is important to recognize the things that are hard for them. A good friendship is one that is reciprocal.

I tried to remember as much and as often as possible that my friends did not have autism in their own life, so I would often remind myself to turn the focus on their own daily life and struggles. (Parent of B)

Another obstacle to building a supportive relationship is when the parents are uncomfortable telling others that they need help. To help extended family members and friends help you, don't be afraid to tell them what you need. Others won't necessarily know that you need help. They may not know what kind of help you need if you don't tell them. Parents worry about asking for help, especially if they have asked for help before. They don't want to abuse the offers to help, but sometimes the challenges of living with ASD may require frequent help. They may feel guilty that they are imposing on the lives of family or friends by accepting help.

The reality is that if people can't help you, they'll tell you. And most people will feel a great sense of relief, even gratitude, when presented with something they *can* do to help. Don't assume that providing help is a burden for the person you ask. All relationships are reciprocal and they wouldn't be actively in your life if they weren't also getting something out of the relationship (Whiteman and Roan-Yager 2007).

> The day I broke down and cried in Conan's preschool after he had screamed getting up, screamed getting dressed, screamed getting into the car, screamed on getting out of it, screamed being carried fighting into school, I think I learned one of life's most valuable lessons: that to admit your vulnerability and let people help is ultimately a sign of strength. It does not mean that the problems disappear but somehow makes them a little less demanding. (Ariel and Naseef 2006, p.114)

In order to receive help, the parents may need to realize that they are not the only ones who can spend time with the child. Parents may need to let go of their worries about allowing others to help with the care of the child. Having someone else take care of the child for brief times can allow parents to get a much needed break and can also help the child develop some flexibility.

> We have found that the most joyful and resilient parents are those who don't try to go it alone. They are skilled at forming,

cultivating, and celebrating their children's connections to other people. (Whiteman and Roan-Yager 2007, p.131)

Parents can teach their relatives or friends the basic skills they need to understand the child and take care of him when the parents are not around. They don't necessarily need to do everything just like the parents do, but it would help for them to understand the child's likes and dislikes and any routines that are important to the child. Parents should share with potential babysitters any strategies to use if the child should get upset.

It is also important for parents to acknowledge the feelings of their family members and friends. They too may be having difficulty accepting the diagnosis.

I felt sad and mad. Why did this have to happen to such a wonderful family who had already gone through a lot in their lives? At the time, I had a son who was healthy and it made me feel almost guilty that he was healthy and her son wasn't. (Friend of a parent)

Parents need to remember that relatives and friends don't always react the way they would like them to. Parents shouldn't judge the relationship by the initial response family or friends may have to the news. Parents need to be patient and understanding and recognize the limitations of others. Some may be quick to adapt to the news and will be ready to support you right away. Others might need more time to adapt.

Parent advocacy is not always about facing opposition. Family members may lose patience. Friendships may feel the strain... Recognizing the limitations of others and learning to compensate for them is a constant requirement. But we have a powerful motivation: the autistic children we love. (Martin 2010, p.72)

Sometimes parents may sense that certain friends or family members are distancing themselves. They may never hear from a particular friend. Or they may find they aren't getting invited to go out and get coffee as often as they used to. One immediate reaction parents may have is to think that the friend is trying to avoid them. The reality may be, however, that the parents' lives have become so busy and crazy with therapies and appointments and managing their child with ASD that the parents have out of necessity started distancing themselves first. The friend may actually be feeling as ignored as the parents feel. Or the friend may be giving the parents space because they think they need that. Before reacting negatively, parents should think about all the factors that may surround the situation and reach out and tell the friend that they miss them.

Unfortunately, some family members or friends may have difficulty offering support or may respond in ways that aren't helpful. If parents find themselves in that situation, they can do certain things. They can be prepared to respond to negative comments with some basic information about the child's ASD. They can also be honest with the family member or friend and let them know when their comments or reactions aren't helpful and when they are. Parents can also be patient as their family members and friends learn about ASD and their child.

In Amy Baskin and Heather Fawcett's book, *More Than a Mom: Living a Full and Balanced Life When Your Child has Special Needs* (2006), they list some rules for parents to follow to develop and maintain their friendships. We could all benefit from using some of these strategies.

- Give your friends time to appreciate your reality: Give them information about the disorder to help them understand.

- Recognize that there are different roles your friends may play in your life: Not all friends need to be aware of your day-to-day challenges. Friends from work, church, book clubs, etc. may not need to know all the details.

- Cultivate friendships both inside and outside of the special needs world: Different perspectives and experiences can enrich your life.

174

- Remember that everything is relative: Neurotypical families have their own challenges that may be different from yours, but are challenging just the same. Most families live with some kind of ongoing stress.

- Communicate well: Misunderstandings may happen. You may think a friend is rejecting you when they are just "giving you space."

(Baskin and Fawcett 2006, pp.41–4)

Chapter 6

ADJUSTING TO LIFE WITH ASD

Raising a child with ASD can be difficult. It requires adjustments and sacrifices on the part of all family members. There are going to be crisis periods and times when every parent feels overwhelmed (O'Brien and Daggett 2006). Parents, and the family members and friends who care about them, are going to find different strategies to manage their stress and adapt to their lives following the diagnosis. It may take longer for some to adjust than others. Some parents and family members may become overwhelmed with grief and some find this experience as an opportunity for inspiration and hope. How you accept this turn of events in your life can be influenced by many factors.

The severity of a child's disability alone does not determine how well a family accepts and adjusts to the child's disability. The adjustment cycle is affected by many factors: the way in which the information was delivered, the family's financial status at the time the disability is identified, how stable the marriage is, what kind of emotional support is available from family and friends, how secure an individual feels about him/herself, how many other children there are, the state of their spirituality, and countless other factors. (Brower and Wright 1986, p.9)

Every family member will have their own way of coping with stress and challenges. Some will be more problem focused and will use the problems they encounter to motivate them into action. Some will be more emotional in how they cope and will want to express their needs openly to others. Others will consider their family problems as very private and keep them to themselves. And some family members when faced with challenges will immediately look for support from their family, friends, and professionals (O'Brien and Daggett 2006).

Coping well requires parents and family members to be patient with themselves and the child. It takes time to understand the disorder and to understand the child with ASD. It takes time to accept the changes in your family's life. Difficult feelings can resurface from time to time and some days may be harder than others. The child with ASD will make strides but will also have occasional setbacks. Family members have to learn to appreciate each small victory the child accomplishes and try not to be disheartened when improvements are slow. Realizing that this is a process is part of coping successfully.

It might be easy for me to suggest what you should or shouldn't do to adjust to living with ASD. I have the benefit of hindsight and the advantage of having made lots of mistakes that I've learned from over the years. I usually learned the hard way what was difficult and what prevented me from being able to accept my child and my family's situation. I also have the benefit of having worked with hundreds of families over the years and have seen what worked (and didn't work) for many of them. I realize that it is not so easy for those of you reading this to immediately embrace the advice and strategies that I will be giving you. I am not in your shoes and my struggles may not be the same as yours. What is most important is that you recognize that adapting is a process, it takes time, and you will adjust by using the strategies most comfortable for you.

ROADBLOCKS TO ADJUSTMENT

Before talking about what can help, it is necessary to discuss some things that may not help. Some of these points came up during our discussion on living with ASD but it is important to mention them again. It is easy to be overwhelmed, especially early on, with trying to find the answer to why your loved one has ASD. It is very normal to have this response. But focusing too much on the "whys" and the "what ifs" can interfere with reaching a point of acceptance and adjusting successfully to the situation. In most cases there will never be a legitimate answer to why this happened. And we can't undo what happened before the child was born or before they were diagnosed. Everyone has regrets about what they wish they had done or known sooner. Focusing on helping the child and moving forward is a more productive use of your time.

Moving forward should include trying not to compare the child with ASD to other children, and instead, focusing on the child's strengths and the improvements they are making. This is very difficult for most people to do. It is an automatic response for us, especially mothers, to compare our children to our friend's children. It can be very painful to watch the child with ASD behave differently than the other children in their preschool class or see them struggle at an activity that seems so easy to others.

These painful feelings are not unique to parents. If you are a grandparent you may be hearing stories from your friends about their grandchildren. You may be feeling sad that your grandchild is not having the same experiences or that you are not able to have the same kind of relationship with your grandchild. There is no magic solution to make this pain go away. When you catch yourself making comparisons, you can, however, remind yourself of all the improvements your loved one is making and how special that child is in your life. Over time you will learn to appreciate all the many wonderful things about the child that can and should be celebrated.

Another behavior that may make it difficult to adapt and cope with this experience is worrying too much about the future. Again, it is a normal response to be scared about the child's future and what it may hold. It's okay to have some concerns about the future because that helps drive us to prepare the child and prepare ourselves for what may be coming. However, worrying too much and making predictions about the future can paralyze our ability to move forward. We can't possibly predict what the child will be like, what they will be able to accomplish, and where they might be in the future. As I have said before, children with ASD are lifelong learners. There are many kinds of support and therapies the child may receive over the years that will help them improve and adapt. There is no way to predict how far they will be able to go. The best thing we can do is prepare for the near future and try not to look too far ahead.

I worried about the transition to middle school for my son with ASD for years before he actually went there. I knew that the social world of middle school and the academic expectations would be huge challenges for him. I worried what adolescence would bring during those middle school years and what new issues or behaviors I would face with my son. The transition to middle school and his years there were difficult at times but it was nowhere near the disaster I imagined. Eric's transition through adolescence was also easier than I imagined. Dealing with his brother's and sister's adolescence was actually more difficult! The point of this story is that I was making myself sick worrying about things in the future that I couldn't possibly predict.

As mentioned in Chapter 2 on living with ASD, many family members feel guilty about something related to their loved one's diagnosis. Either they feel they should have known sooner, or should have done something differently. They may feel guilty about the choices they made or didn't make. It is easy to become so overwhelmed with guilt that it is difficult to move forward and accept the child and the circumstances of your life. None of us is a perfect parent and none of us has a crystal ball that can tell us what we need to do for the absolutely best outcome for our child. Each person does the best with what they have and makes the best decisions they can. Part of adjusting to your life is to trust your instincts and not beat yourself up about what you can't do, physically, financially and emotionally, to help your child. We are all only human.

ESTABLISHING MORE
CONTROL OF YOUR LIFE

One of the stressful aspects of having a child with ASD is the unpredictability and loss of control that parents can experience. Not understanding ASD, not understanding the child's behavior, not knowing what to do, and not knowing what the future will hold, all contribute to that sense of insecurity and life being out of control. Even if things feel out of control, however, there are choices parents (and family members and friends) can make that influences what happens next and encourages a sense of empowerment and control over your life.

You can choose to learn more about the disorder, which can in turn help you feel more confident and in control of what's going on in your life. Becoming knowledgeable about ASD can help with the confusion and frustration you may be feeling. It can also make you a more competent advocate for the child. Personally, it helped me to learn everything I could and I attended many conferences and trainings about ASD and developmental disabilities. I also read everything I could find about autism. However, reading lots of information about ASD may be too overwhelming for some people. You may want to find one or two books or one or two websites to read to minimize the confusion that can come from trying to absorb too much.

You can also take more control over your life by choosing to connect with others who are going through similar experiences. Reading personal accounts about living with autism or meeting other families is often very helpful. There is comfort in knowing that you are not alone and that others know what you are going through. Finding others who share similar concerns and experiences can help you cope with the emotions you are experiencing. Groups of other parents of children with ASD can provide an opportunity to feel less isolated and to learn from the experiences of others. Other families living with ASD can connect you to resources in your community and help with problem-solving. Connecting with others can also be helpful for extended family members and friends. Getting involved within the autism community can help to broaden your circle of support.

I've known parents over the years who are not as interested in sharing their personal lives and reaching out to other family members of ASD. They may not feel comfortable connecting with others when they are struggling to sort out their own feelings following the diagnosis. That's okay. Do what you feel comfortable doing and don't push yourself to do things you aren't ready to do. You'll know when you are ready to connect with others going through similar situations.

I remember inviting a friend whose child was recently diagnosed to a local family support group. I was receiving so much inspiration and support from being with other families that I assumed this would also help my friend. There were many families at the event and many individuals with ASD, children and adults, with varying levels of challenges. Being around older individuals with ASD and individuals with many challenges was too overwhelming to my friend. As the parent of a very young, newly diagnosed child, she was not ready to think about the possible future for her child. It made her incredibly sad and she ended up deciding to leave the event. I felt badly that I may have added to her grief. It taught me that every parent is going to adjust differently and in their own time.

Another choice parents can make to regain more control over their lives is to focus on helping the child with ASD. As I mentioned earlier in the book, some parents will focus their energies on finding all the available services and resources to help their child. They may spend lots of time going online, making phone calls, visiting programs and schools and setting up therapy appointments. While this can be very time consuming, it can also help the parent feel like they are doing something at a time when they don't know what to do. Similarly, some parents choose to immerse themselves in working one-on-one with their child. At a time when you don't know what the future holds, helping the child learn new skills can make the parent feel that they have some control over the child's future.

Finding all the available services to help the child and working with the child can help parents feel more confident. Additionally, the knowledge gained from these activities helps the parent become a better advocate for the child. When you know the system and know the child's strengths and challenges, you are better able to speak up for them when needed. Advocating is an extremely important role for parents and one they will play throughout the child's life. If you are a family member or friend to parents of a child with ASD you can help support their advocacy efforts and become involved with them as an advocate in the autism community.

Many family members of individuals with ASD will feel the need to share what they have learned and give something back to others. Giving back can take many different forms such as sharing your wisdom and experiences at local support groups or advocating for the rights of individuals with ASD in your community or at the state or federal level. Sometimes giving back can be very small and personal such as giving a supportive smile or comment to a parent struggling with an out-of-control child in the mall (Whiteman and Roan-Yager 2007). Getting involved in helping others gives us a focus beyond the difficulties of our own situation and can add meaning to our lives. It can make us feel better as we hope that we can make others feel better too.

> The key here is the phrase, "when we are able." If we are in crisis, or our situation is fresh, putting our energy outside ourselves and our families may not be appropriate. Sometimes helping our children is all we can do. But when the time is right, using our gifts to create a better world goes a long way in helping create our *own* happier, more joyful life. (Whiteman and Roan-Yager 2007, p.196)

BUILDING A SUPPORT SYSTEM

In Areva Martin's book, *The Everyday Advocate: Standing Up for Your Child with Autism or other Special Needs* (2010), she suggests that families can develop empowerment circles as a way to cope and to help the child. Circles could include family members, friends, and professionals who offer expertise, insight, and experience to help the family. A family's empowerment circle might include the professional who originally evaluated the child, a neighbor, the pastor, a social worker, or other parents and family members and friends who want to be involved in the child's life. This team can offer practical advice and emotional support as well as help in problem solving as issues come up for the family (Martin 2010).

Empowerment circles, or whatever you may call them, can be a great way of building the support that a family will need, not only when the child is young but also over time. Keep in mind that the support system you build for yourself does not have to have an official name or have regular meetings to be helpful. Your support system may include a few close friends and family members you can go to for advice and support when needed. It may include a particular professional who understands your child and knows the system you need to navigate. The members of your support system may also change over time as you make new connections and develop different needs. What's important is that you have people who can help you get through difficult times.

> I am grateful to have women in my life...who listen well, offer support, and sometimes challenge me. Being able to talk about my feelings, no matter how difficult, is crucial if I want to work through my fears and hurt. Acceptance of my situation comes from being honest, heard and loved. (Whiteman and Roan-Yager 2007, p.160)

TAKING CARE OF YOURSELF

Another important part of coping with living with autism is to take care of yourself. Parents may be so busy with taking care of the needs of the child that they don't allow themselves time to relax, cry, or just think. Extended family members and friends also may be busy worrying about the child and forget to take care of themselves through this process of adjustment. Taking short walks and practicing deep breathing or meditation exercises can help. Adding pleasure to everyday tasks is important, such as listening to music while cleaning your house or listening to a book on tape when riding in the car. Taking a relaxing bubble bath or having a glass of wine with dinner are little things you can do to pamper yourself during a stressful time.

Taking care of yourself needs to include finding time for a break now and then, asking for help when you need it, and talking to someone who understands who can support you. If you don't have anyone available that you can talk to, consider keeping a journal. Sometimes just the process of putting your thoughts on paper can be very cathartic. I've known several parents who have kept journals, especially during difficult times, and it helped them a lot. They ended up going back later and reading what they had written and were helped by seeing how far they and their child had come. Some people enjoy contributing to autism-related blogs, freely sharing their thoughts and emotions. There are numerous chat rooms and websites where you can find others in similar circumstances.

Being able to laugh at the absurdity of your life can also be a healthy way to cope. Laughter triggers chemical reactions that release endorphins and make us feel better. It also decreases the release of stress-producing hormones (Marshak and Prezant 2007).

Sometimes you just have to laugh. As the father and primary caregiver of a young man with autism, I've learned over the years that laughter can be a way to cope with difficult times. The ability to find humor in offbeat moments, to laugh at funny experiences, can soothe the weary soul and release the stress that comes from living every day with autism. At times, it seems the only thing that keeps me afloat and carries us into the future is humor. (Sell 2007, p.68)

Over the years, my son has helped me appreciate the importance of having a good sense of humor. He is often brutally honest and sometimes says things that probably shouldn't be said out loud. On the morning of New Year's Day, I was sitting at the kitchen table having breakfast with my son and my sister and her husband. To appreciate the humor in this story it is important to point out that my sister and her husband are missionaries and my brother-in-law is a pastor. Eric, then 28 years old, decided to announce to everyone at the table what his New Year's resolutions were this year. I was excited that Eric was initiating a conversation, something he rarely does. He proudly announced: "I want to get my driver's license and get laid!" Needless to say, we all were at a loss for words.

Obviously there are a variety of strategies you may choose from to cope or adapt to the changes ASD has brought to your life. The goal of adjusting is to reach the point of accepting the child for who they are and not who we expect them to be. This takes time and involves relinquishing our expectations of normal development and our obsessions with "fixing" the child. It involves finding the strengths in the child and learning to celebrate them. It also involves not dwelling on the failures, but instead learning from them and setting new goals.

I discovered that my understanding of "who Eric is" can change. I have always prided myself on being knowledgeable about autism and being the expert on my child. But I have learned recently that no matter how much I think I know about my child and how his autism affects him, he can and probably will surprise me. Eric has always been socially withdrawn, preferring to be alone, and I thought he would be that way forever. Now he is surprising me every day with ways he is reaching out socially and the new interests he is developing as an adult. Seeing how he has changed, I have learned not to close any doors simply because I think my son won't go there (Palmer 2006).

Our ability to accept our child and accept our life with ASD can also fluctuate over time. One day you may feel very accepting of the uniqueness of your child and your life. You may have no trouble finding the positives in this experience and being very optimistic about the future. Other days, or around particularly important events or milestones, it may be more difficult to find this level of acceptance. I hope that the harder days will remind you to appreciate the days when your feel at peace with your life and with your child.

DEALING WITH THE PUBLIC

Another part of coping is learning to deal with the public or those people who don't know anything about you or the child who has ASD. From the grocery store, the local McDonald's, the church or synagogue you may attend, etc. we are regularly revealing our lives with autism to those around us. Families of children with ASD soon realize how powerful words can be. From the parent of Sam, who has autism:

> During my pregnancy with Paul, I was waiting at the supermarket checkout with Sam screaming around my ankles, when the old lady in front of me said "And you want more?" More than two years on and I still get comments about his occasionally appalling behavior. No one seems to look at us and think that my son requires special understanding. Instead, I get all sorts of comments that question my competence as a mother, leaving me feeling that it is a cold and unpleasant world out there. (Ariel and Naseef 2006, p.93)

Most families have an experience in public, or something said to them about their child with ASD, that they will *never* forget. And sometimes it's not just what people say to the parents but what they don't say. The icy stares or the rolling eyes can be just as painful to endure as words. In order to fully understand what living with ASD can be like, family members and friends need to appreciate how hurtful the reactions from strangers can be. Not every adventure into a public place will result in a bad experience of course, but many will.

As was mentioned before, disclosing to close family members and friends can be difficult for parents. Disclosing to strangers or people you only have a brief connection with can be even more difficult.

> During the five years since the diagnosis that changed our world, Elliot and I have both been learning to talk. His few words are all the more valuable for being so rare, and I have learned to say "autism" and "disability" without flinching. I have acquired polite phrases that I can trot out whenever

> I need the world to give my son a break... I can now be
> composed as I excuse my precious boy; but, oh my, it's been a
> long, hard journey. (Sell 2007, p.62)

It is important to remember that disclosure about the diagnosis or about the child's challenges does not have to be an "all or nothing" decision. Parents don't have to tell everyone; they may only choose to tell those people who need to know the most. And when telling people, they don't have to quote the definition of autism in the DSM-IV or name the diagnostic criteria for ASD. Sometimes a brief, general description is enough, such as "he has a learning difference," or "she has a language delay," etc. Whatever is most comfortable for that person to say is okay.

This parent suggests a solution that many parents might agree would be helpful:

> I have been very embarrassed in public over my son's behavior
> to the point where I wished I had a sign on my back that said,
> "Don't worry, this is normal. My son is autistic." I have heard all
> the remarks; I have sensed the animosity from acquaintances
> and strangers. (Myers *et al.* 2009, p.681)

Sometimes disclosing with words is too difficult in a public place, especially if the child is having a meltdown and the parent is embarrassed or upset. Many parents find it helpful to have cards to hand out to people who are giving them dirty looks or making rude comments. The cards may say something like

> I apologize if my child was disturbing you. Autism is a
> neurobiological disability affecting about 1 in every 110
> children born today. Behavior that may on the surface seem
> rude is my child's ONLY way of dealing with the world. If
> this is the first time autism has touched your life, I hope you
> will be patient and understanding. (Gallagher and Konjoian
> 2010, p.68)

Parents constantly have to decide who they should tell or not tell about their child's problems. If their child "blends," they may not have to say anything to the people around them. But at times the child with ASD may exhibit behaviors that stand out or attract people's attention.

Sadly, people with autism often face social disapproval—not because they look different, but because they look so "normal." Unlike other disabilities, autism doesn't clearly disable a person on the outside. (Shore and Rastelli 2006, p.335)

Telling others is particularly difficult when your child has an invisible disability, such as ASD, and others aren't immediately able to see their differences.

I'm afraid if I tell people about his disability, they'll get to know his "label" before they get to know him. (Gallagher and Konjoian 2010, p.64)

Parents often worry that disclosing and naming what is different about their child will make others treat them differently. In my own situation with my son, I have found that the "label" is stigmatizing only if it is not accurate or if it is used to limit that child's opportunities. The reality is that people may already sense your child is different and sometimes it may be better to educate others rather than letting them come up with their own explanation that will most likely not be accurate. Every time we tell someone about ASD, it means there is one more person who can educate others and help break the stigma about autism.

I don't just go out and tell people that Jake has autism, but I also think it's important to educate the general public. So if we're out and people try to engage Jake in conversation then look to me as to why he is despondent, I will tell them that he is on the spectrum. (BabyCenter 2011)

It is tricky dealing with the unhelpful responses of others. Sometimes we may respond better than other times depending on how we feel at the time and how important that person is to us or to the child. Parents can at times feel angry toward even well-meaning people. Antoinette, a parent of a son with Down syndrome, explains:

> If one more parent comes up to me and says "Oh, you are SO blessed…" I swear I'll knock them over! (Baskin and Fawcett 2006, p.104)

We know most unsupportive comments are made by people who don't understand and have limited knowledge about ASD. But parents or others who care about the child may not always want to be responsible for educating others.

> Most people do not understand the difficulty in taking a child with ASD out in public. We have had very negative experiences with judgmental people. They see a little girl that is crying and pitching a fit and because she looks normal they think that a "good spanking" would fix her. If only!!! I have become thick skinned and learned to tell people that she is autistic and did not choose and cannot help that, but they are rude and judgmental and they *should* be able to help that. (Autism Speaks 2009, p.2)

It is important to have a plan for how to respond to others who are not being helpful when you are in public. Being informed and able to respond with information about ASD is one option. It can also help to prepare a set of responses to use in stressful situations that you can just say and not have to create at a difficult time. You can be prepared with an escape plan to use in case a difficult situation arises, just ignore the person's comments and walk away.

Whatever is said or done, stay calm and try to put the situation into perspective. If people have negative feelings about your child, that is their problem. It's okay to be honest about your feelings and tell people that what they did or said is hurtful. It may also help to have someone to vent to after the fact; a friend you can call and tell what happened and how angry or hurt you felt.

It is also important to remember that when parents feel vulnerable they can be hypersensitive to criticism from others. Sometimes they can read things into other people's reactions that are not what was intended at all. People's reactions may indicate surprise or curiosity rather than the disapproval or judgment we may imagine. Other people may actually want to help, but are unsure how to do so (Morrell and Palmer 2006).

In conclusion, the important thing to remember is that unpredictable behaviors happen sometimes in public, whether they are our child's behaviors or the behaviors of well-meaning or rude strangers. Knowing this, we can prepare ourselves to respond to the situation and come armed with strategies to escape or defend, whichever is necessary in that particular situation. Sometimes we will handle it well and sometimes we'll have regrets and wish we had handled it better. Over time it does get a little easier and we become "thicker skinned" and more able to handle the comments or responses of strangers and can begin to look at these experiences as learning opportunities.

Chapter 7

TOP TEN TIPS FOR FAMILY MEMBERS AND FRIENDS

You may have picked up this book and thought, "This could really be helpful information to me, but when do I find the time to read it?" This chapter is for those of you who could benefit from an abbreviated version of some of the more important recommendations given in this book. Of course I still hope you will find the time to read the entire book because it will help in your understanding and the support you can offer. This list of top ten tips is primarily for the extended family members and friends who want to understand and help the family living with ASD. However, it is also for parents of children with ASD. Each tip includes suggestions for parents to help them build good supportive relationships with their family members and friends.

1. LISTEN

- Be a good listener. Allow the parents to speak about their feelings. Encourage them to share what they are going through. Try not to give advice or to make judgments. Just allow them to talk and be there to listen.

- Control the urge to always try to make the parents feel better. Allow them the opportunity to complain sometimes. Be that "safe person" they can talk to.

- Keep asking questions and keep listening because the family's needs will fluctuate and change over time.

For parents

Your family members and friends can't listen if you aren't sharing. Be open with them about what you are going through. You don't have to do this alone.

2. LEARN

- Educate yourself about ASD and learn how it affects your loved one. Ask questions, read books or online information, or get involved in a local autism group.

- Try not to make judgments based on assumptions or too little information. ASD is a complicated disorder and looks different in every child.

- Learn how to interact with your loved one with ASD. Find out what they like and dislike. Ask the parents what strategies are helpful in interacting with the child.

For parents

Help your family members and friends learn what they need to know to understand ASD and your child. Share information with them. Educate them about your child's challenges and strengths.

3. EMPATHIZE

- Try to understand the day-to-day life of the family and the child. When you understand more about living with ASD, you will know what kinds of support the family needs.

- Recognize when the family is dealing with more difficult situations such as new behavioral challenges or times of big changes or transitions, and offer your support.

- Appreciate even the smallest improvements and celebrate the child's accomplishments with the family.

For parents

Your family and friends can't empathize if they don't know what living with ASD feels like. Share what is difficult and what is inspiring about your life with your child with ASD.

4. ACCEPT

- Accept the child with ASD for who they are and show that you care about them.

- Understand and accept the changes that ASD has brought to the family's life. Put judgments aside and respect the parents to know what is best for their child.

- Grieve for any lost expectations you may have had and move on. Think about the ways that knowing the child has added to your life.

For parents

When you accept your child for who they are, your family and friends will be more likely to accept them too. Help them see what you love so much about your child.

5. REACH OUT

- Offer what you can to help. Any offers are helpful whether it is practical support (like running errands, babysitting, bringing meals) or assisting the family financially, or through emotional support.

- Ask the parents what they need, and if they can't answer, suggest your own ideas of ways you can help.

- Understand that the need for support is long term and not just when the child is young.

For parents

Allow people to help you. Your family and friends want to support you and don't know how. Be honest about what helps and doesn't help.

6. BE FLEXIBLE

- Accept that some family traditions or routines may need to be adjusted to facilitate including the family living with ASD.

- Try to adapt to the needs of the family. Make things as easy as possible for them to be included.

- Understand when complications arise and be supportive.

- Learn to accept and appreciate the child's different way of thinking and learning.

For parents

Be open with your family and friends about what is difficult and what changes they can make to include your family. Recognize that you may need to be flexible as well.

7. COMMUNICATE

- Be open about your feelings and let the parents know when you have questions. It is okay to say you are sad or don't know what to do.

- Tell the parents when you think they are doing a good job. Let them know you respect them and the choices they are making for their child.

- Be careful about giving advice when it hasn't been asked for. You can communicate your support without trying to "fix" the problem.

For parents

Be open and allow others to share their concerns or questions. Reach out to family members and friends who seem to be distancing themselves and let them know that you miss them.

8. BE INVOLVED

- Be a part of the family's life. Invite them to family gatherings and social events or spend time with the family in more informal settings. If there are siblings, be involved in their lives too.

- Support the events the family may be involved in within the autism community.

- Remember that you don't have to live near the family to stay involved. Call or email regularly and ask how things are going. Follow the child's progress and celebrate his or her achievements.

For parents

Include your family members and friends in your life. Make it easier for them to be involved by communicating often, sharing information and inviting them to family or community events.

9. FORGIVE

- Understand that everyone is trying their best to deal with a difficult situation.

- Understand that in stressful situations, mistakes can be made. When a parent's emotions are high, they may not be as sensitive to the feelings of others.

- When feelings are hurt, talk about it openly and honestly and don't let too much time go by. Apologize or forgive. Your relationship is too important to lose.

For parents

Recognize how difficult it is for others to know what to say and do. First reactions from others may be based on emotions, confusion, and a lack of information. Be honest about what is helpful and what isn't. Appreciate every offer of support.

10. TAKE CARE OF YOURSELF

- Give yourself time to grieve and adjust, just as the parents had to. Recognize that this is a process and there will be good and bad days.

- Seek out your own support. Reach out to others who care or who know what you are going through.

- Discover what helps you deal with stress and recognize the importance of taking care of yourself.

For parents

Validate the feelings your family and friends may be having. Recognize how difficult this is for them too. Encourage them to reach out for support too.

HELPFUL BOOKS
AND WEBSITES

There are thousands of books and websites related to ASD. These are just a few of the books and websites I would recommend to parents, family members, and friends.

INTRODUCTORY BOOKS
ABOUT ASD

Sicile-Kira, C. (2010) *41 Things to Know about Autism.* Nashville, TN: Trade Paper Press.

The author provides a clear, instructive explanation of autism. If you know someone with autism and would benefit from a quick, straightforward explanation of the condition, this book is for you.

Notbohm, E. (2005) *Ten Things Every Child with Autism Wishes You Knew.* Arlington, TX: Future Horizons.

The book defines the top ten characteristics of children with autism. It is a guide for all who come in contact with a child on the autism spectrum.

Shore, S.M. and Rastelli, L.G. (2006) *Understanding Autism for Dummies.* Indianapolis, IN: Wiley.

This reassuring guide explains the symptoms of autism, how it's diagnosed, and the current options for treatment. You'll get helpful information on the latest in genetic and biomedical research, as well as coverage of special needs financial planning, legal rights for education, and handling issues unique to adults with autism.

BOOKS FOR PARENTS

Whiteman, N.J. and Roan-Yager, L. (2007) *Building a Joyful Life with Your Child Who Has Special Needs*. London: Jessica Kingsley Publishers.

Drawing from their own experiences of parenting children with special needs, interviews and workshops with parents, and research findings, the authors explore practical ways in which parents can develop a resilient and positive attitude towards caring for their child with special needs.

Stone, W.L. and DiGeronimo, T.F. (2006) *Does My Child Have Autism? A Parent's Guide to Early Detection and Intervention in Autism Spectrum Disorders*. San Francisco, CA: Jossey-Bass.

This groundbreaking book, by two of the foremost experts, teachers, and clinicians in the field, provides a guide for parents about what to look for at home at 24 months or even earlier, what to do, and how to get the right kind of help from doctors, counselors, therapists, and other professionals.

Morrell, M.F. and Palmer, A. (2006) *Parenting Across the Autism Spectrum: Unexpected Lessons We Have Learned*. London: Jessica Kingsley Publishers.

Winner of the Autism Society of America's Outstanding Literary Work of the Year in 2007, this book offers a personal perspective and practical guidance for parents at the start of their journey with autism. The authors share their experiences of parenting children at opposite extremes of the autism spectrum.

Ozonoff, S., Dawson, G., and McPartland, J. (2002) *A Parent's Guide to Asperger Syndrome and High-Functioning Autism: How to Meet the Challenges and Help Your Child Thrive*. New York: Guilford.

From leading experts in the field, the book is packed with practical ideas for helping children relate more comfortably to peers, learn the rules of appropriate behavior, and participate more fully in school and family life.

Klass, P. and Costello, E. (2003) *Quirky Kids: Understanding and Helping Your Child Who Doesn't Fit In—When to Worry and When Not to Worry*. New York: Random House.

Written by two pediatricians, this book takes you through the stages of a child's life, helping to smooth the way at home, at school, even on the playground.

BOOKS ABOUT ADVOCACY

Shore, S.M. (ed.) (2004) *Ask and Tell: Self-Advocacy and Disclosure for People on the Autism Spectrum*. Shawnee Mission, KS: Autism Asperger Publishing.

Ask and Tell aims to help people with autism effectively self-advocate in their pursuit of independent, productive and fulfilling lives. It is unique in being the first book to speak to the twin issues of self-advocacy and disclosure for people with autism and by consisting exclusively of contributions by those on the autism spectrum for persons on the spectrum.

Martin, A. (2010) *The Everyday Advocate: Standing Up for Your Child with Autism or Other Special Needs*. New York: New American Library (Penguin).

Nationally recognized expert on autism advocacy, Areva Martin shares her hard-won knowledge as a parent of an autistic child and an individual rights attorney. In *The Everyday Advocate*, she lays out vital and relevant step-by-step instructions to parents facing the seemingly impossible odds of advocating for a child with autism.

Wright, P.W.D. and Wright, P.D. (2008) *Wrightslaw: From Emotions to Advocacy—The Special Education Survival Guide*, 2nd edn. Hartfield, VA: Harbor House Law Press.

This is a great resource for parents and family members. It will teach you how to plan, prepare, organize, and get quality special education services. Whether you are new to special education or an experienced advocate, this book will provide a clear roadmap to effective advocacy for your child.

PERSONAL ACCOUNTS
BY INDIVIDUALS WITH ASD

Shore, S.M. (2003) *Beyond the Wall: Personal Experiences with Autism and Asperger Syndrome*, 2nd edn. Shawnee Mission, KS: Autism Asperger Publishing.

This honest, courageous book, written by a person with high-functioning autism and Asperger syndrome, draws on personal and professional experience and is a touching and, at the same time, highly informative book.

Willey, L.H. (1999) *Pretending to be Normal: Living with Asperger's Syndrome.* London: Jessica Kingsley Publishers.

The author is an individual with Asperger syndrome and the mother of a daughter with AS. Liane Holliday Willey shares, with insight and warmth, the daily struggles and challenges that face many of those who have Asperger syndrome.

Grandin, T. (2006) *Thinking in Pictures: And Other Reports from My Life with Autism,* 2nd edn. New York: Vintage (Random House).

Grandin delivers a report from the country of autism. Writing from the dual perspectives of a scientist and an autistic person, she tells us how that country is experienced by its inhabitants and how she managed to breach its boundaries to function in the outside world.

PERSONAL ACCOUNTS BY PARENTS

Paradiz, V. (2005) *Elijah's Cup: A Family's Journey into the Community and Culture of High-Functioning Autism and Asperger Syndrome.* London: Jessica Kingsley Publishers.

This is a powerful story of the author's own struggle with her son Elijah's Asperger syndrome. Valerie Paradiz's inspiring narrative offers compelling insights into daily life with Elijah and her own "shadow syndrome," which affects many family members of autistics. It is also a celebration of the idiosyncratic beauty of the Asperger mind and the sense of mutual support and self-respect in the ASD community.

Hughes, R. (2003) *Running with Walker: A Memoir.* London: Jessica Kingsley Publishers.

With disarming honesty and humor, the book tells how a family copes and keeps hope alive despite the staggering difficulties autism presents.

Park, C.C. (1982) *The Siege: A Family's Journey into the World of an Autistic Child.* New York: Back Bay Books.

At age two, in 1960, Jessy Park was withdrawn, unable to walk or talk, yet oddly content within the invisible walls that surrounded her. The study of autism was still in its infancy. This powerfully moving book, now widely regarded as a classic work, charts a surprising journey of discovery as it records the challenges and rewards of the first eight years of Jessy's life.

BOOKS HELPFUL FOR GRANDPARENTS, SIBLINGS, AND OTHER FAMILY MEMBERS

Martin, E.P., Jr. (1999) *Dear Charlie: A Guide for Living Your Life with Autism.* Arlington, TX: Future Horizons.

In this heartwarming book, a grandfather offers loving advice in a series of letters to his grandson Charlie, who has autism. His letters educate and inspire, while painting a beautiful, positive portrait of children with autism. He explains what autism is and what it is not, offers social dos and don'ts, and encourages Charlie to be who he is and follow his dreams.

Thompson, C.E. (2009) *Grandparenting a Child with Special Needs.* London: Jessica Kingsley Publishers.

When a new baby is born into a family, grandparents are excited about having a baby to enjoy and love. If the child is born with a disability, it can be difficult to know how to react and how best to help the child and the family as a whole. This book provides guidance on how to grandparent a child with special needs and give every grandchild the love and care they deserve and parents the added support they need.

Johnson, J. and Van Rensselaer, A. (2010) *Siblings: The Autism Spectrum Through Our Eyes.* London: Jessica Kingsley Publishers.

This collection of personal stories has been written by siblings for siblings, and each individual tale comes directly from real-life experience, offering everything from empathy and constructive advice to reassurance that occasional feelings of resentment and embarrassment are entirely normal. This book is essential reading for children and teenagers with a sibling on the autistic spectrum, and for parents wishing to understand how autism in the family will affect their neurotypical child.

Harris, S.L. and Glasberg, B.A. (2003) *Siblings of Children with Autism: A Guide for Families.* Bethesda, MD: Woodbine House.

Takes an in-depth look at what it is like to grow up as a sibling of a child with autism. This book addresses a full range of questions and concerns, including how to explain autism to siblings, how to help siblings share their feelings, and how to balance the needs of the entire family.

Ariel, C.N. and Naseef, R.A. (eds) (2006) *Voices from the Spectrum: Parents, Grandparents, Siblings, People with Autism, and Professionals Share Their Wisdom.* London: Jessica Kingsley Publishers.

This is a compelling collection of personal accounts from people on the autism spectrum and those who care for them, including professionals, friends and family members. The contributions tell of both the positive and negative effects of autism on individuals and families.

Santomauro, J. (2009) *Your Special Grandchild: A Book for Grandparents of Children Diagnosed with Asperger Syndrome.* London: Jessica Kingsley Publishers.

This book offers a fun and accessible introduction for the grandparent of a child diagnosed with AS. *Your Special Grandchild* addresses questions or concerns that grandparents might have, such as "What are the characteristics of AS?" "How did my grandchild get AS?" and "What happens now?" Also included are activities to help grandparents come to terms with and move forward from a diagnosis of AS, and work together with the family to support the child.

BOOKS ON ADULT ISSUES

Perry, N. (2009) *Adults on the Autism Spectrum Leave the Nest.* London: Jessica Kingsley Publishers.

This book takes a comprehensive look at the problems facing adults on the autism spectrum, and offers real solutions to those problems. This is a great resource for parents, family members and professionals with an interest in helping people on the autism spectrum to develop meaningful adult relationships and lead their lives with a sense of dignity and independence.

Grandin, T. and Duffy, K. (2004) *Developing Talents: Careers for Individuals with Asperger Syndrome and High-Functioning Autism.* Shawnee Mission, KS: Autism Asperger Publishing.

This book gives hard-hitting, concrete help for adolescents and young adults preparing for the adult world of work, and for the parents and educators who are helping them.

Zaks, Z. (2006) *Life and Love: Positive Strategies for Autistic Adults*. Shawnee Mission, KS: Autism Asperger Publishing.

This book was written for adults on the spectrum and for involved parents, spouses, and friends. The author describes and suggests concrete ways to deal with some of the issues and problems faced by those on the autism spectrum. She also includes a broad spectrum of suggestions for different types of relationships and weaves these together with the core concept of self-esteem.

Palmer, A. (2006) *Realizing the College Dream with Autism or Asperger Syndrome: A Parent's Guide to Student Success*. London: Jessica Kingsley Publishers.

This book is both a practical and a personal account of one ASD student's successful experience of going to college. This book is essential reading for any parent considering college as an option for their child, disability service providers in colleges, and for ASD students themselves.

HELPFUL WEBSITES

All websites were accessed on November 4, 2011.

General information and resources in the United States
Autism Society of America

www.autism-society.org

Includes an interactive map to use for searching for support groups and chapters across the United States. Also provides an online resource directory to search for resources in your area.

Autism Speaks

www.autismspeaks.org

Includes a downloadable 100 day kit created specifically for newly diagnosed families to make the best possible use of the 100 days following their child's diagnosis of autism or AS/HFA.

Centers for Disease Control and Prevention

www.cdc.gov/ncbddd/autism/index.html

Includes a very thorough related links page with links to more information on education, screening, financial resources, research, etc.

General information and resources in Europe

National Autistic Society (UK)

www.autism.org.uk

Lots of articles available on the site including articles specifically for grandparents and other family members and self-advocates.

Autistica (UK)

www.autismspeaks.org.uk

Formally closely affiliated with Autism Speaks in the United States, this organization raises funds for biomedical research into the causes and treatment of autism.

Autism Europe

www.autismeurope.org

Autism Europe is a liaison among more than 80 member associations of parents of persons with autism in 30 European countries.

Autism Independent UK

www.autismuk.com

Includes many Temple Grandin articles and the excellent booklet called *How To Understand People Who Are Different* by Brad Rand.

General information and resources in Australia

Autism Spectrum Australia (Aspect)

www.autismspectrum.org.au/a2i1i1l4451487/welcome.htm

Australia's largest not-for-profit, autism specific service provider. Includes support and information for families.

Raising Children Network:
The Australian Parenting Website

http://raisingchildren.net.au

The complete Australian resource for parenting newborns to teens. The site includes a Parenting Children with Autism page with numerous articles, links to resources, and a way to link to discussion forums with other parents.

Autism Queensland

www.autismqld.com.au/index.php?page_id=49

Site includes general information about autism and resources and under "Useful Information" has links to Australian autism organizations and other Australian resources.

General information and resources in Canada

Autism Society Canada/Société canadienne de l'autisme

www.autismsocietycanada.ca

Includes a searchable Canada-wide directory of ASD services and related supports.

Autism Speaks Canada

www.autismspeaks.ca

Includes list of websites for families.

Health Canada/Santé Canada

www.hc-sc.gc.ca/hc-ps/dc-ma/autism-eng.php

Under "Health Concerns" this website includes a page on autism with links to many Canadian organizations.

Other helpful websites

Autism Network International

www.autreat.com

A self-help and advocacy organization run by and for autistic people.

Autism Society of North Carolina Bookstore

www.autismbookstore.com

Largest non-profit ASD-specific bookstore in the United States. Provides personalized service by telephone or email.

Coulter Video

www.coultervideo.com

This site features videos, articles, and other resources to help people with Asperger syndrome and autism deal with the world—and to help others in the world understand and appreciate them.

Do2Learn

www.do2learn.com

The mission of Do2learn is to use technology and the web to provide special learning resources for individuals with disabilities and the professionals, and caregivers who serve them. Working with leading educators, clinicians, teachers, and parents, we develop serious games and learning material targeting specific deficits of individuals with neurological disorders including ASD.

National Dissemination Center for Children with Disabilities (NICHCY)

http://nichcy.org

A central source of information on disabilities in infants, toddlers, children, and youth. Includes lists of every state's resources.

OASIS @ MAAP

www.aspergersyndrome.org

OASIS (Online Asperger Syndrome Information and Support) has joined with MAAP Services for Autism and Asperger syndrome to create a single resource for families, individuals, and medical professionals who deal with the challenges of Asperger syndrome, autism, and pervasive developmental disorder—not otherwise specified (PDD-NOS).

Schafer Autism Report

www.sarnet.org

Online daily newspaper about ASDs. Almost all news appearing in print about ASDs ends up on this site.

Siblings of Autism

www.siblingsofautism.com

This website was created by a sibling of a child with ASD and is for siblings of autistic children. Includes good information and useful links.

Wrightslaw

www.wrightslaw.com

Gives accurate, reliable information about special education law, education law, and advocacy for children with disabilities.

REFERENCES

American Psychiatric Association (APA) (2000) *Diagnostic and Statistical Manual of Mental Disorders* (DSM-IV-TR). Washington, DC: APA.

Ariel, C.N. and Naseef, R.A. (2003) *The Relationship Factor: When Special Needs Challenge a Household.* Available at www.autismsupportnetwork.com/news/relationship-factor-when-special-needs-challenge-household-133245, accessed on June 11, 2011.

Ariel, C.N. and Naseef, R.A. (eds) (2006) *Voices from the Spectrum: Parents, Grandparents, Siblings, People with Autism, and Professionals Share Their Wisdom.* London: Jessica Kingsley Publishers.

Autism Society of America (2009) *Facts and Statistics.* Available at www.autism-society.org/about-autism/facts-and-statistics.html, accessed on July 18, 2011.

Autism Speaks (2009) *Interactive Autism Network Research Report: Family Stress— Part 3.* Available at www.autismspeaks.org/inthenews/ian_findings_family_stress_part_3.php, accessed on June 9, 2011.

BabyCenter (2011) *Telling Friends about Your Child's Diagnosis.* Available at http://community.babycenter.com/post/a27394201/telling_friends_about_your_child's_dx, accessed on May 13, 2011.

Baskin, A. and Fawcett, H. (2006) *More Than a Mom: Living a Full and Balanced Life When Your Child has Special Needs.* Bethesda, MD: Woodbine House.

Brill, M.T. (1994) *Keys to Parenting the Child with Autism.* Hauppauge, NY: Barron's Educational Series.

Bristol-Power, M. (2000) "Research in autism: New directions." *The Advocate,* July–August, 16–17.

Brodey, D. (2007) *The Elephant in the Playroom: Ordinary Parents Write Intimately and Honestly about Raising Kids with Special Needs.* London: Plume (Penguin).

Brower, D. and Wright, V.K. (1986) *The Rubberband Syndrome: Family Life with a Child with a Disability.* USA: Iowa Department of Public Instruction and Nebraska Department of Education.

Centamore, M.G. (2009) "Understanding parents of children with autism." *Pathways to Family Wellness 21.* Available at http://icpa4kids.org/Wellness-Articles/understanding-parents-of-children-with-autism.html, accessed on April 1, 2011.

Centers for Disease Control and Prevention (CDC) (2010a) *Autism Spectrum Disorders: Data and Statistics.* Available at www.cdc.gov/ncbddd/autism/data.html, accessed on May 13, 2011.

Centers for Disease Control and Prevention (CDC) (2010b) *Facts about ASDs.* Available at www.cdc.gov/ncbddd/autism/facts.html, accessed on May 13, 2011.

Centers for Disease Control and Prevention (CDC) (2010c) *Treatment.* Available at www.edc.gov/ncbddd/autism/treatment.html, accessed on May 13, 2011.

Connolly, J., Reitzel, J.A., Szatmari, P., and Harrison, A. (2011) "Innovations in Assessing Cognition in Nonverbal Children with Autism Spectrum Disorder." International Meeting for Autism Research. Available at http://imfar.confex.com/imfar/2011/webprogram/start.html, accessed on February 6, 2012.

Copeland, A. (2011) *Being Friends to Parents of Children with Autism: While You May Not Be Able to Relate, You Can Still Offer Support.* Available at www.associatedcontent.com/article/1001370/being_friends_to_parents_of_children.html?cat=25, accessed on April 24, 2011.

Covey, S. (1997) *The Seven Habits of Highly Effective Families.* New York: Golden Books.

Davis, N.O. and Carter, A.S. (2008) "Parenting stress in mothers and fathers of toddlers with autism spectrum disorders: Associations with child characteristics." *Journal of Autism and Developmental Disorders 38,* 7, 1278–1291.

Diamont, M. (2010) *Autism Reshaping Grandparent Role, Survey Finds.* Available at www.disabilityscoop.com/2010/02/19/grandparents-autism-survey/7054, accessed on April 13, 2011.

Donnelly, J.A., Bovee, J-P., Donnelly, S.J., Donnelly, L.K., *et al.* (2000) "A family account of autism: Life with Jean-Paul." *Focus on Autism and Other Developmental Disabilities 15,* 4, 196–201.

Early Signs of Autism (2010) *What is the Global Incidence of Autism?* Available at www.earlysignsofautism.com/what-is-the-global-incidence-of-autism, accessed on August 1, 2011.

Exkorn, K. (2005) *The Autism Sourcebook: Everything You Need to Know about Diagnosis, Treatment, Coping, and Healing.* New York: HarperCollins.

Featherstone, H. (1980) *A Difference in the Family: Life with a Disabled Child.* New York: Basic Books.

Frith, U. (ed.) (1991) *Autism and Asperger Syndrome.* Cambridge, UK: Cambridge University Press.

Gallagher, G. and Konjoian, P. (2010) *Shut Up about Your Perfect Kid: A Survival Guide for Ordinary Parents of Special Children.* New York: Three Rivers Press (Random House).

Ganz, M.L. (2007) "The lifetime distribution of the incremental societal costs of autism." *Archives of Pediatrics and Adolescent Medicine 161,* 343–348.

Glasberg, B.A. and Harris, S.L (1997) "Grandparents and parents assess the development of their child with autism." *Child and Behavioral Therapy 19,* 2, 17–27.

Grandin, T. (1995) *Thinking in Pictures: And Other Reports from My Life with Autism.* New York: Vintage (Random House).

Harris, S.L. and Glasberg, B.A. (2003) *Siblings of Children with Autism: A Guide for Families.* Bethesda, MD: Woodbine House.

Hastings, R.P., Kovshoff, H., Ward, N.J., Espinosa, F.D., Brown, T., and Remington, B. (2005) "System analysis of stress and positive perceptions in mothers and fathers of pre-school children with autism." *Journal of Autism and Developmental Disorders 35,* 5, 635–644.

Janzen, J.E. (2003) *Understanding the Nature of Autism: A Guide to the Autism Spectrum Disorders,* 2nd edn. Austin, TX: Hammill Institute on Disabilities.

Kanner, L. (1943) "Autistic disturbances of affective content." *Nervous Child 2,* 217–250.

Katz, S. and Kessel, L. (2002) "Grandparents of children with developmental disabilities: Perceptions, beliefs, and involvement in their care." *Issues in Comprehensive Pediatric Nursing 25,* 2, 113–128.

Klass, P. and Costello, E. (2003) *Quirky Kids: Understanding and Helping Your Child Who Doesn't Fit In—When to Worry and When Not to Worry.* New York: Random House.

Larson, E. (1998) "Reframing the meaning of disability to families: The embrace of paradox." *Social Science and Medicine 47,* 7, 865–875.

LeVine, R.A. (1988) "Human Parental Care: Universal Goals, Cultural Strategies, Individual Behavior." In R.A. LeVine, P. Miller and M. West (eds) *Parental Behavior in Diverse Societies: New Directions for Child Development, No. 40.* San Francisco, CA: Jossey-Bass.

Levy, S. (2003) "Complementary and alternative medicine among children recently diagnosed with autistic spectrum disorder." *Journal of Developmental and Behavioral Pediatrics 24,* 6, 418–423.

Marshak, L.E. and Prezant, F.P. (2007) *Married with Special-Needs Children: A Couple's Guide to Keeping Connected.* Bethesda, MD: Woodbine House.

Martin, A. (2010) *The Everyday Advocate: Standing Up for Your Child with Autism or Other Special Needs.* New York: New American Library (Penguin).

Mauro, T. (2011) *After the Diagnosis: You've Made the First Step. Here Are Six More.* Available at http://specialchildren.about.com/od/gettingadiagnosis/a/diagnosis.htm, accessed on April 13, 2011.

Meadan, H., Halle, J.W. and Ebata, A.T. (2010) "Families of children who have autism spectrum disorders: Stress and support." *Exceptional Children 77,* 1, 7–36.

Meyer, D.J (1995) "Siblings of children with special needs: Programs, services and considerations." *National Bulletin on Family Support and Children's Mental Health 9,* 2, 8–10. Research and Training Institute for Human Services, Portland State University.

Miller, N. (2002) *Nobody's Perfect: Living and Growing with Children Who Have Special Needs.* Baltimore, MD: Brookes.

Morrell, M.F. and Palmer, A. (2006) *Parenting Across the Autism Spectrum: Unexpected Lessons We Have Learned.* London: Jessica Kingsley Publishers.

Mozes, A. (2008) *Health Needs of Autistic Children Often Unmet.* Available at www.healthscout.com/template.asp?page=newsdetail&ap=1&id=621768, accessed on June 8, 2011.

Myers, B.J., Mackintosh, V.H., and Goin-Kochel, R.P. (2009) "'My greatest joy and my greatest heart ache': Parents' own words on how having a child in the autism spectrum has affected their lives and their families' lives." *Research in Autism Spectrum Disorders 3,* 3, 670–684.

National Institute of Mental Health (NIMH) (2008) *Autism Spectrum Disorders (Pervasive Developmental Disorders).* Available at www.nimh.nih.gov/health/publications/autism/complete-index.shtml, accessed on May 13, 2011.

Notbohm, E. (2005) *Ten Things Every Child with Autism Wishes You Knew.* Arlington, TX: Future Horizons.

O'Brien, M. and Daggett, J.A. (2006) *Beyond the Autism Diagnosis: A Professional's Guide to Helping Families.* Baltimore, MD: Brookes.

O'Machel, P. (2011) *Grandparents to Special-Needs Children Pulled in Two Directions.* Available at www.chicagoparent.com/magazines/special-parent/2011-spring/grandparents-to-special-needs-children-pulled-in-two-directions, accessed on April 13, 2011.

Ozonoff, S., Young, G.S., Carter, A., Messinger, D. *et al.* (2011) "Recurrence Risk for Autism Spectrum Disorders: A Baby Siblings Research Consortium Study." *Pediatrics 128,* 3, e488–e495.

Palmer, A. (2006) *Realizing the College Dream with Autism or Asperger Syndrome: A Parent's Guide to Student Success.* London: Jessica Kingsley Publishers.

Prescott, B. (2011) *New Therapy Helps Nonverbal Children With Autism to Say First Words.* Available at www.bidmc.org/News/InResearch/2011/October/MusicTreatsAutism.aspx, accessed on February 6, 2012.

Powell, T.H. and Ogle, P.A. (1985) *Brothers and Sisters: A Special Part of Exceptional Families.* Baltimore, MD: Brookes.

Powers, M.D. (ed.) (1989) *Children with Autism: A Parent's Guide.* Rockville, MD: Woodbine House.

Rackley, J. (2011) *Extraordinary Dads, Special Kids: Meeting the Needs of Special Needs Children.* Available at www.specialkidstoday.com/articles/parenting-strategies/meeting-the-needs-of-special-needs-children-4718, accessed on June 10, 2011.

Reinberg, S. (2011) *Autism Takes an Economic Toll on Mom's Job.* Available at http://health.usnews.com/health-news/family-health/brain-and-behavior/articles/2011/05/11/autism-takes-an-economic-toll-on-moms-job-income-study, accessed on June 30, 2011.

Rudy, L.J. (2009a) *How to Get Dad More Involved with His Child with Autism.* Available at http://autism.about.com/od/familyissuesandautism/f/fatherinvolved.htm, accessed on June 10, 2011.

Rudy, L.J. (2009b) *Readers Respond: Your Tips for Grandparenting a Child with Autism.* Available at http://autism.about.com/u/ua/copingwithautism/USGrandparent.htm, accessed on April 13, 2011.

Rudy, L.J. (2010) *Grandparents and Autistic Children.* Available at http://autism.about.com/od/familyissuesandautism/f/grandsonFAQ.htm, accessed on April 13, 2011.

Rudy, L.J. (2011) *Top Ten Treatments for Autism.* Available at http://autism.about.com/od/treatmentoptions/tp/topdevandbehav.htm, accessed on April 13, 2011.

Sandler, A.G., Warren, S.H., and Raver, S.A. (1995) "Grandparents' adjustment to children with disabilities." *Educational Gerontology 21,* 3, 261–273.

Schall, C. (2000) "Family perspectives on raising a child with autism." *Journal of Child and Family Studies 9,* 1, 409–423.

Scherman, A. and Gardner, J.E. (1995) "Grandparents and grandchildren with special needs: A unique relationship." *Focal Point: A National Bulletin on Family Support and Children's Mental Health,* Fall, 1–7.

Sell, C. (ed.) (2007) *A Cup of Comfort for Parents of Children with Autism: Stories of Hope and Everyday Success.* Avon, MA: Adams Media.

Seltzer, M.M., Greenberg, J.S., Orsmond, G.I., and Lounds, J. (2005) "Life course studies of siblings of individuals with developmental disabilities." *Mental Retardation 43*, 5, 354–359.

Sharpley, C.F., Bitsika, V., and Efremidis, B. (1997) "Influence of gender, parental health, and perceived expertise of assistance upon stress, anxiety, and depression among parents of children with autism." *Journal of Intellectual and Developmental Disability 22*, 1, 19–28.

Shore, S.M. and Rastelli, L.G. (2006) *Understanding Autism for Dummies.* Indianapolis, IN: Wiley.

Sicile-Kira, C. (2004) *Autism Spectrum Disorders: The Complete Guide to Understanding Autism, Asperger's Syndrome, Pervasive Developmental Disorder, and Other ASDs.* New York: Berkeley.

Siegel, B. (2008) *Getting the Best for Your Child with Autism: An Expert's Guide to Treatment.* New York: Guilford Press.

Simons, R. (1987) *After the Tears: Parents Talk about Raising a Child with a Disability.* Denver, CO: Children's Museum of Denver.

Sinclair, J. (1993) "Don't Mourn for Us." International Conference on Autism, Toronto. Available at http://ani.autistics.org/dont_mourn.html, accessed on June 8, 2011.

Stillman, W. (2010) *Parenting Children with Asperger Syndrome: Extended Family.* Available at www.netplaces.com/parenting-kids-with-aspergers-syndrome/family-dynamics/extended-family.htm, accessed on April 24, 2011.

Stone, W.L. and DiGeronimo, T.F. (2006) *Does My Child Have Autism? A Parent's Guide to Early Detection and Intervention in Autism Spectrum Disorders.* San Francisco, CA: Jossey-Bass.

Tilton, A.J. and Thompson, C.E. (eds) (2004) *The Everything Parent's Guide to Children with Autism: Expert, Reassuring Advice to Help Your Child at Home, at School, and at Play*, 2nd edn. Avon, MA: Adams Media.

University of Florida Health Science Center (2005) *Autistic Kids Benefit from Dads' Involvement.* Available at http://newswise.com/articles/view/510950, accessed on June 10, 2011.

Whiteman, N.J. and Roan-Yager, L. (2007) *Building a Joyful Life with Your Child Who Has Special Needs.* London: Jessica Kingsley Publishers.

Zachry, A.M. (2008) *Extended Family Members' Emotions in Special Education: Emotions Part 5—Extended Family.* Available at www.kps4parents.org/blog/?p=31, accessed on April 1, 2011.

INDEX